"Breathing Again"

He thought he'd keep me bound, broken and destroyed

Copyright © 2017 Genie Santos

All rights reserved. No part of this book may be used or reproduced by any means, graphics, electronic, or mechanical. Including photocopying, recording, taping or by any information storage retrieval system without the written permission of publisher except in the case of brief quotations embodied in critical articles and reviews.

I have tried to recreate events, locales and conversations from my memories of them. In order to maintain their anonymity in some instances, I have changed the names of individuals and places, I may have changed some identifying characteristics and details such as physical properties, occupations and places of residence.
Scripture quotations are taken from **HOLY BIBLE***, New Living Translation, New International Version, King James Version, Amplified Bible New King James Version.*

Printed in U.S.A
ISBN 978-1982056629

Dedication

*To every abused minister who has had to keep quiet!
To every woman facing tough decisions.
You can breathe again !*

Acknowledgements

Special thanks to Rev. Mercedes Valentin, who God placed in my life to stop me from quitting and being there by my side when many others left me. Your love for the broken healed me. Thank you for being my pastor, friend, sister and kingdom partner.

And to all those family and friends who stood by me during the storm. All those who opened their homes and hearts to me. Thank you.

Lastly, my sister, Assoc. Pastor Marilou Rivera, thank you for praying me through always. My cousin, Carolyn Rivera who helped me pick out cover design on a long Amtrak ride to Florida. Book Author, Nellie Escalante, you encouraged me not to put this project away but move forward with it. And all those who kept praying and helping me press through.
I love you all!

Introduction

As a Minister, I have come across so many broken marriages, many abused women and even men. We as ministers' counsel, pray and lead the people. We want the best for those who have entrusted us with the matters of their hearts. However, some situations tends to be more difficult than others. But what happens when it hits home? When it happens to you. I didn't know what hit me. I saw the red flags but I stood, believing the prophetic words, believing I could be his hero and save him from his pain. Feeling shameful, being mocked by him and his circle, trying to hide from others that this new marriage was hell on Earth and the pain was killing me inside, trying to prove to myself I could handle this and that someday he would change. Nevertheless, I winded up in a situation where I almost lost myself. I had experienced this in the past but why again? And why is it worst? Wasn't he a minister? Why was he abusing me? Why did he hate me this much? How can he preach after cursing at me and beating me? Wasn't I good enough for him? Why was I making excuses for his behavior? It was a painful three years that seemed like 30. I felt isolated for a while like a bird trapped in a cage. Yet, through it I learned many lessons about love, kindness, forgiveness but I also learned about how much I'm worth. I learned this wasn't my portion, not for me or for any woman. I also now have a new viewing angle toward domestic violence in the church, the secrets behind the pulpits and the pressures to keep it quiet. I pray the pages of this book brings you revelation. Bring you

have been or are being abused freedom. Bring you the abuser repentance and freedom , brings the church the conviction and boldness to stop sweeping domestic violence in ministers' lives under the carpet and brings you the minister clarity and the strength and compassion to help others to breathe again!
Pastor Genie Santos.

Chapter Index

1. Where do I begin?
2. The problem with guarding my heart!
3. The Elephant in the Room
4. Egg Shells Underneath my Feet
5. Watch out for that glass!
6. Prince turned frog!
7. To love or to detox?
8. When is Enough, Enough?
9. Wrinkled Table Placemats
10. How far could he go to create an alibi?
11. An unending cycle I needed to end
12. The Controller
13. Journey through the truth
14. Abandoned or Released?
15. Plan to Breathe Again
16. He thought he'd keep me bound, broken and destroyed

Prepare your hearts for what you're about to read.

Father God touch the hearts and minds as they ready the pages of this book. Pour conviction where conviction is needed. Bring peace to a troubled heart, solutions for their situation. Bring clarity Lord and deliver those that are bound, broken and feeling destroyed.

In Jesus name
Amen

Chapter 1 Where do I begin?

Writing is a wonderful thing to me. It's such a wonderful form of expression whereby I exercise the freedom of writing inspirational materials that can be used as witnessing tools, but writing about certain events in my life has been the biggest challenge. Yet, I know that a piece of me is most likely a piece of you my dear reader. I can assure you Life hasn't been easy but one thing I can say is that God has brought me a long way, He has big things in store for me and He has big things in store for you too. But we must believe and sometimes we're too busy looking at what's in front of us or picking on our old scabs and not letting ourselves to be healed and therefore delaying the process, delaying the blessing and the purpose.

I have had so much in my heart for several years now, I didn't know which one of my book projects I wanted to finish first. I was quite unsure of what God wanted me to unveil first and who's hearts would be ready to receive. Full of so much of me to share that I was waiting to burst at the seams and so I began to pour out inspirational writings to steer people to greater heights. However, if you read all my other books intensively, you'll figure out that they all have pieces of things I've experienced at some point in my life. Much of the wisdom I carry was attained through my own life and not through books. But this book that you have begun to read is a bit different. It will give you a glimpse at a painful time in my life and how God delivers and restores. Though I didn't understand then what I understand now and I can testify God brought me out from an abusive marriage.

No, this wasn't my first marriage, this was my second marriage, supposed to be my last. But what took 10 to 15 years to happen in the last marriage took just three months to begin in this one. You see that saying "hurt people hurt people" is very real. I had married the most charming, elegant, talented man but he had a dark painful past which he had not allowed God to heal him from and so I winded up being his punching bag. There is no excuse for anyone to abuse anyone but here I was and didn't know how to come out of it. Before I go on, let me say that when God has a plan, you must stick to His timing, His plan and purpose and that comes with obedience. I was set apart for the Lord but my eyes went on man.

Though, we both knew the word and tried to do things right as it was our desire to wait till marriage, we opened a can of worms by giving into our desires. We winded up burning with passion, now there was a pregnancy (yes indeed – I can hear the sounds of the critics reading this …whispering to one another, easy there) and we jumped into marriage. It was done privately and quickly, but as quickly as that came as quickly the first slap came as well.

He cried, he felt bad that first time but it didn't stop him from doing it again and again.

Things got crazy, miscarriages, abuse, hate, infidelity, anger, rage, lies, isolation, and mockery followed suite. Our life was crazier than the soap operas he enjoyed watching. (Novelas) sometimes, I wondered if he wanted to live out the scripts. I spent several time trying to figure his pain out. What was the root of it? Was it his mother? Was it his father? Was it this? Was it that? And next thing I knew I was trying to figure out where's Genie? How did I wind up here? How do I keep this pain a secret? How can I ever confront the world again? This man's pain turned him into an abuser, and I pleaded to God, fasted, sought his face, and sought for counsel. Some ministers told me to run and I didn't understand why they didn't tell me to fight. Others kept telling me to stay and fight and I didn't understand why I had to stay in this battle. So confused, I tried to make sense of it all and have compassion. I thought of all he had shared with me about his growing up. The abandonment and rejection and I felt responsible as a wife and a Christian to fight. I took up a burden that wasn't mine. I knew I wasn't the first woman who had been abused by him.

But I cannot speak for those other women's experiences only for what I've heard but even though I heard, I thought that I could give him a chance of redemption that I'd be different because Jesus is the forgiving Lord and I loved him enough to think that my love will heal him. Big mistake! I would look at every red flag waving high but maybe I just didn't want to be alone anymore, maybe it was the dream of marrying a man that would be my ministry partner and was used by God and preached the gospel. Maybe my dream was so big that it blinded me and I just wanted it to be him, maybe it was that I believed every prophetic word but was every prophetic word from God? When God speaks, He's accurate. But anyway it didn't get easier and no matter what I did to please him, it didn't work and I walked on egg shells all the time. Even praying out loud bothered him.

I lost my identity, I lost friends, and I lost family. Don't get me wrong, I believe your real friends will stick by you no matter what your choices are to be right next to you but a lot of my so-called friends decided to walk away. They hated the fact that I was going through the storm but they failed to open an umbrella to shelter me from it.

It's at moments like these you learn so much about yourself, about people and about God. It is under pressure where you find out what you're made of.

Some things are in our lives because we put them there and some things are there to try your walk in the lord. Before this all began to happen to me, I was walking on water so to speak. The ministry was thriving but my heart deeply deceived me. My heart told me don't wait, this is it go for it, and my spirit said wait on the Lord. I awoke love before its time and now when I found myself under pressure at first, I began to sink like a submarine, my smiles hid the brokenness and I had no idea how to escape this.

But Before I go further speaking about my experience, I want to speak to you. Yes, you who is reading this, maybe you're in an abusive relationship or maybe you're the abuser. I pray God's presence invades your space right now and that clarity comes into your heart and mind.

We often make excuses for ourselves and when the pressure comes on we find out how many dents we have in our armor. We're afraid to fight for our hearts and our minds and a biblical principle that we so often put to the side to Guard our hearts above all things and to claim that sound mind which God has given us.

. Proverbs 4:23 New Living Translation (NLT)
23 Guard your heart above all else,
    for it determines the course of your life.

2 Timothy 1:7 New King James Version (NKJV)
7 For God has not given us a spirit of fear, but of

power and of love and of a sound mind.
Until you understand these two scriptures fully you'll be going around in circles.
Let's look at the word guard for a moment. According to the Merriam – Webster Dictionary Guard is defined as :

a : a defensive state
b : a defensive position (as in boxing)

a : the act or duty of protecting or defending
b : the state of being protected : protection

It is our duty, our responsibility to GUARD OUR HEARTS! In guarding our hearts, we will find direction from the Lord for that's when his perfect love cast out all our fears and we can have the sound mind needed in making tough decisions. It's easier to tell someone to get out of a bad situation but how easy is it for those in it? That's why I unveil many things in this book to help you who find yourself bound by the deceit of your heart, the opinions of others and the intimidation of the abuser to take a deep breath and be set free!

Write your thoughts.

Notes :

_____

How can you or someone you know relate to this last chapter ?
For your own reflection :

_____

Chapter 2

The problem with guarding my heart!

Because there was such a need and thirst of being loved by someone in my life and I had been struggling with feelings of rejection and abandonment that came from my past, I opened up the gates of my heart too quickly. We all know that it's important to guard our heart and the scripture is specific of the why. We must Guard our hearts because it determines the course of our lives.
In allowing myself to be vulnerable, transparent and opened so quickly, I didn't see the road that it would lead me to. All I knew was I'm available, he's available, we are feeling each other and God spoke. Wait God spoke! Yes He did. As a matter of fact, one of the underlined key words I heard so often was DON'T RUSH! I remember ministering at a church in Spanish Harlem and the Pastor of the house pulled me to the side and said to me "Sister Genie, the Lord shows me this is your husband." But she was in tears and I'm talking about tears of affliction not joy. I had already received that word twice about him, but again it seemed like the DON'T RUSH was deleted or I had selective hearing. As she gave me the word, I took a look at her and I see pain in her eyes and she was hesitant but there she said "He's the one, but please don't rush. If you do you will experience great heartache." He's not ready! That stood with me, I knew I had began to see certain red flags, I knew he

was somewhat complicated, but I had been reached by old friends who also knew him telling me, Genie, nooooo! He has abused other women. But I just kept looking at the fact that God makes all things new and that is a truth. Yet, I could see that truth was not manifested in his life. It didn't matter how long he was in the church, didn't matter if he was ordained, didn't matter if he sang beautifully. And here was the Holy Spirit trying to get me to hit the breaks, be still, wait and pray. However, my heart wanted it now. When you don't guard your heart it becomes deceitful, it believes every thought and process that was not deposited by the right spirit.

Jeremiah 17:9 New Living Translation (NLT)

9 "The human heart is the most deceitful of all things, and desperately wicked.
Who really knows how bad it is?

Seriously now, that's deep. It is described as the most deceitful of all things. This is why God tells us to guard our heart. In which direction will the course of life take you if we don't guard our hearts? I'm amazed even as I share this on how the word of God describes it as the most deceitful of all things. Not some things but ALL things and to top it off desperately wicked!

Wicked indeed when not holding the purposes of God. When a heart is guarded it's positioned like a boxer. When a heart is guarded your shield of faith is not down it automatically goes up. Faith is not carrying your shield dangling on the side. Your spiritual reflexes move quickly in discernment. But the flesh wants what the flesh wants and I wanted to be loved, I wanted it then, I felt I deserved to be happy, I wanted that husband and I fell in love with this man's imperfections, I embraced his flaws after all I told myself isn't that what God wanted me to do, why is everyone now judging him for his past? Let him live. I didn't see it wasn't judgment rather they were waving flags, neon signs, smoke signs and they were shouting, Genieeeee, there's a truck coming, get out the wayyyyyyyy!!!

But there is something else I want to point out extensively. When a person is totally convinced about someone or something, the most powerful thing you can do is pray for them, love them and get them to trust you by just being there. When the heart has been left unguarded the ears aren't going to listen to anything that tells it otherwise. In my case, I felt people were judgmental of his person and some were envious of the relationship since I had been harassed even by people from his past via anonymous calls and so forth. I wasn't in the position to hear anyone with their opinions, I wasn't even adding one thing with the other, I rather kept my cool. It was obvious if this much drama was going on in the beginning what would be of me marrying him. Now, let's take a look at the words desperately wicked in that bible verse I just shared a few moments ago. My heart was desperate, my heart was quite desperate as insecurities and fears of loss took over. I had lost love in the past and I was afraid of losing it again, I was also looking at my age. I was 42 years old and was not getting any younger, I had so many thoughts of confusion running through my head. I thought to myself maybe he is it , he's the one, why should I wait? Eventually, we both couldn't control our passions and when passions aren't submitted to God everything that is not of God begins to kick in. This carried us into a marriage that was reckless. I played the hero while he played the victim's role. I submitted myself to the point of not caring about anything else but this obsessive thought of saving him. It began so subtle, I thought I was doing right in staying. Besides, I tried to walk away, he tried to walk away too but we always ran back to one another after each drama. Romantic right? No, it was unhealthy because there were no changes and this carried in major problems as we proceeded to get married. But I was taken and engulfed by his charm, his ability to raise kids on his own, his talents, even his freckles were adorable. I ignored how he spoke about every woman that had been significant in his life as I thought well maybe they were evil. I bought all his sobs on how God forgave but men didn't. I bought in his victim mentality and allowed my heart to deceive me. Does this sound familiar to you? Is your heart unguarded? Has your heart been exposed to deceit and the wickedness that comes with it? Are you dating someone showing signs of an abuser?

Quick note: According to an article written by Bonnie Koehn in the Huffpost:

One of the reasons women get caught up in unhealthy relationships is that abusers can be very charming. They can appear confident, attentive and sweet, and they have this intoxicating energy when pursuing a woman.

Perhaps, you already took the plunge and got married. You were probably as convinced as I was that you had this under control and that the world was just hating on you both and now you're hitting the bottom of the sea, oxygen leaving you too embarrassed to tell anyone and those you turned to threw an anchor on you. That's a rough place to be at. But give me your hand at this moment, come on, don't feel silly, stretch your arm out in faith, I'm stretching mine out to grab you. It's time to pull you up my friend, you will definitely breathe again!

A pause of prayer :

Lord open up the spiritual understanding of this wonderful reader . Wipe the tears of this broken person reading and make them whole.

Lord equip your leaders to fight against this ugly monster of abuse.

In Jesus name ...

Chapter 3

The Elephant in the Room

The average size of an elephant varies among African and Asian Elephants. The height of an African elephant is about 2.5 to 4 meters and Asian Elephants are 2 to 3 meters tall. The African elephants weighs up to 2,268 to 6,350 kilograms, while Asian Elephants weighs up to 2,041 to 4,990 kilograms.
Liveanimalslist.com

How can one not see an elephant in a room? Imagine that! Seems impossible right? It is! Yet, in our lives there are issues as big as an elephant slapping us right in the face, but we choose to ignore it or we are literally blinded by our emotions and we don't see it. We don't get the picture and though it's swinging its trunk right in front of us as we remain oblivious. I will never forget that spring in 2013, what a bittersweet season. The obvious elephant was in the room but I was concerned with doing what was supposedly the right thing by fixing the situation. We had already indulged in passion and had consequences. We had gotten engaged back in February, which was very surprising due to the fact he broke up with me a few days prior to that day. Everything was a yo-yo going up and down like a frantic haunted elevator ride. But my heart wanted what it wanted. Forget about the words DON'T RUSH! We messed up and we both wanted to fix this. Of course, I always had some haters down the

road, doesn't everyone at some point? But not a bad reputation though for I was known for kingdom purposes. But he had a terrible reputation many were aware of. It was so bad that he got banned for a couple of years from certain churches. But again, my mentality was, I'm not going to judge him. His past doesn't define him and that's true for all who let go of their past and live in righteousness. But the obvious was he was still not only holding on to his past, he was always repeating patterns in his life. I knew this but the Wonder Woman syndrome was deeply rooted in me. I really thought I was on some life's mission. I really was convinced if this was my husband, then it didn't matter if we had sinned because we repented and would get married, though I was told to slow down, but we already went there, we had premarital intimacy and so marriage was the direction we chose. . One Monday he said to me, "Genie, we are getting married on Friday." He added it had to be private and that he wanted to honor me and didn't want my reputation tarnished like his, but it had to be done privately for this is the way he felt from the Lord plus he didn't want anyone calculating wedding date and pregnancy. He didn't want any of his exes to sabotage us and so forth. I just heard he wanted to get married, he wanted to honor me. Never mind the elephant! But little did I know that later on it would be an avenue to persecute me. It wasn't going to be just some yelling at me, which of course was verbal, mental and emotional abuse but he would also rise up to try to destroy my character.
Everything that week went so well. Things were

supernaturally provided. God extended His mercy to us, I cannot deny He didn't. He saw beyond our stupidity and He was dealing with our hearts. But because of the sin we allowed to penetrate us, the door was opened to the enemy. We had both given legal right to hells angels. However, God weighs the heart of man and not once did He leave me as though spring started feeling like an early premature winter in my life. The day came when we tied the knot - I remember feeling so nervous, I thought he wouldn't go through with it. I fasted, I prayed and we went right to the city hall. Strangely, the place was completely empty. We were in and we were out. My sister was our witness. We took pictures, ate, and went back home. No honeymoon because of his pending responsibilities at home with his family and I was ok with that. I just wanted him by my side. I accepted his ways but adapting to all that was a great challenge. The first slap came, the second one came, I had lost my job because I had been out sick and so taking another day off to get married was never an option and I had to bring proof that this is what I was doing . He refused to hand over the marriage license, an argument that emotionally pulled me down and it was the beginning of that heartache I was warned about. We got married on Friday and by Monday, he was threatening to annul our marriage. The stress was quite high as I was without a job, a baby, all dreams got shattered in a matter of weeks. .

A lot happened which was too much to write about at this point. This isn't a tell-all book or a bash a man book. I'm sharing these details so you can see how confused and blind one could become when in love with an abuser and how your life can change in an instant. One decision you make can paralyze you, your dreams, career, or ministry. It can demolish relationships, suppress you, oppress you and take you into a world of twisters, tornadoes and loneliness.

This all goes back to not guarding my heart. Now fear came in, there was love on a one way street, there was confusion, desperation and it felt like I was going to lose my mind. I held on to my apartment in New Jersey I figured out, ok I can stay three days out of four with him in Nj until he and his family adapts to me. See, he didn't prepare his family. One was bedridden and the other one had a disability as well but pretty functional, independent, smart and I guess tired of all the railroad of women that had been through their lives. He didn't want to share anything with his daughter and didn't allow me to share with my kids which were grown as well. But, I thought about it, yep, I began to pay attention to the elephant in the room. At this point, I got backed up with rent, but my brother who's with the Lord now, Tony and my other brother Bill were always looking out for me. My brother Tony said to me, "Sis, don't move in completely, something's not right. Keep this apartment, I'll help you." But my new husband didn't want to hear that. When I told him it was better for me to come a couple of days in the week he said I belonged to him and needed to submit.
He was right. I married him, my place was with him. But now after the incidents that had taken place

immediately after marriage, I was afraid and I wanted to give his daughter time to adjust to me and me to her and also to the rest of the household. The landlord's wife kept getting at me because of the rent and just right when my brother was about to wire me the money, one chatterbox sister in Christ who owned a Christian book store in Nj opened her mouth. See, the landlady worked next door, I guess she was asking her about me and mentioned I was late with rent. Lily the book store owner volunteered information to the landlady. She told her I had just gotten married and I need to be with my husband. The landlady was outraged, because she didn't know my personal life. Lily went as far as giving her my husband's number. Well, what do you think happened? He yelled at me, told me I was un -submissive , foolish and my place was home with him. I couldn't pay them the debt, because he made me tell my brother not to send the money. I was already feeling intimidated, I already had experienced busted bottom lip before. So I obeyed. He put all my things in storage, the deal was he'd help me pay for it and I'd take only what I could use for that season. When I arrived in his 3 bedroom home with 5 closet spaces, I was just told to put my toiletries in the second shelf of his armoire and a hamper to fold my clothes in, just a little corner on his dresser for perfume and a little space in his closet for my shoes. He only hung up my wedding outfit.
I felt like a guest. I didn't feel like a bride. I felt the stinging of my hearts deceit but now I was in it and I had to confront what was to come.

My dear reader, abuse in any form is unacceptable and if you've made the mistake to wind up in a situation that's not full of peace and is scary, you can get up and leave. Don't allow shame, people's opinions, religion, fear keep you there. Once the disrespect, the belittling begins it doesn't stop. Don't set yourself up to failure. Don't punish yourself! Let's keep swimming in this story and don't let go of my hand, believe me I know it's not easy for you, but I know soon you'll be able to feel your heartbeat again…

Notes :
_____

Chapter 4

Egg Shells Underneath my Feet

Have you ever heard that expression "walking on eggshells?" This is what the Cambridge Dictionary defines it as; If you are walking on eggs/eggshells, you are being very careful not to offend someone or do anything wrong:

It seemed to be that anything I did or said was wrong the majority of the time. It felt like I had to hold my breath. I couldn't express anything without it turning into an argument. I was so afraid of turning the switch on him and it becoming worse than what it was. At one point, I wasn't sure if I was married or just joined the military. But I never expressed this to anyone, I'm in this now and I felt I had to deal with it. Besides, I was sure the love of God in me would change his heart. He just needed more time. Well, time was not what he needed, I can assure you that now. Everything I did was never enough, I didn't know what else to do to please this man. I didn't know what else to do to make him feel well, I did everything from modifying the way I dressed to who I spoke to, who I texted, even the time I went to sleep was controlled. Oh, and didn't let him catch me getting up for midnight snacks! That was a no, no in his book! Kitchen was closed off

after bedtime! I of course submitted to the principle out of my obligation to submit as a wife and out of fear. And that led him controlling everything. Now speaking about submission; it is written
Ephesians 5:22-24 New Living Translation (NLT)
22 For wives, this means submit to your husbands as to the Lord. 23 For a husband is the head of his wife as Christ is the head of the church. He is the Savior of his body, the church. 24 As the church submits to Christ, so you wives should submit to your husbands in everything.

This scripture was one of his favorites. Everyday I heard how foolish and unsubmissive I was. His concept of this scripture was so thwarted and he used it to manipulate, intimidate and control me.
Many men use this scripture for those same reasons. It seems to be they read up to verse 24 and not go further. This has caused not only terrible situations of domestic violence in the lives of women in the church body but this mindset has also brought about spiritual abuse from male leaders who until this day and time have no clue of God's calling upon women and their freedom to minister. In some churches, because it's a male authority with no discernment scriptures like these have been misused and misguided women who have come to pour out their hearts in what they thought was a safe place to have peace, but the answer was pray more, fast more, give him more sex, he's a man, men do these things and so forth.

Ladies you cannot submit unto a man who does not submit to God! God didn't call you to bondage, He called you to peace.

Here's something I read that caught my eye in reference to walking on eggshells.

The most insidious aspect of living with an angry or abusive partner is not the obvious nervous reactions to shouting, name-calling, criticism or other demeaning behavior. It's the adaptations you make to try to prevent those painful episodes that defines the situation. You walk on eggshells to keep the peace or a semblance of connection. Women are especially vulnerable to the negative effects of walking on eggshells due to their greater vulnerability to anxiety. Many brave women engage in constant self-editing and self-criticism to keep them from "pushing his buttons." Emotionally abused women can second guess themselves so much that they feel as though they have lost themselves in a deep hole. Emotionally abused men tend to isolate more and more, losing themselves in work or hobbies or anything but family interactions.
"Walking on eggshells" by Compassionpower.com

To the Men: if you have to walk on eggshells and you're constantly feeling you have to prove yourself as a man, you find yourself crying because you're constantly called names and being put down, then you didn't marry a helpmate you married helphate!

Men are abused too! Just wanted to put that out there. I've had many men of God turn to me for advise seeking for my opinion, write to me and witnessed some crying like babies because a woman hurt them. This goes back to hurt people hurt people!

Crunch, crack, crunch there goes them eggshells. No one should live with fear of the person they love. I loved the man I was married to. But I feared him more than I loved him. One time he said to me: I could put you in a body bag, disappear and no one would know it was me!
Going back to previous chapters, my heart had been left unguarded, this left me powerless, unloved and almost losing my mind. But I stood firm. I had to save my face, I had to save this marriage, I was a newlywed and everyone had given up on him. I did all that not realizing I was the one needing to be saved from what was to come!

My friend, take off the cape, the tights, put down the lasso – you can't save an abuser. I hear crunching, cracking again, is that you? Would you quit tippy toing!

C'mon now! I'm with you, EXHALE!

Things to reflect on:

Notes:

Chapter 5

Watch out for that glass!

Ecclesiastes 7:9 New Living Translation (NLT)
9 Control your temper,
    for anger labels you a fool.

I remember one of my Pastors once asked a question during a preaching. What do you get when you tilt over a glass of orange juice? That message stood so embedded in me, it never left my memory. I bring the same question to my congregants today. Obviously we all know the answer to that
Question. Whatever the glass is holding is what's gonna spill out from it. If it's orange juice that's what's gonna spill, if it's milk that's what's gonna spill and so forth. The word of God tells us:
Luke 6:45 New International Version (NIV)

45 A good man brings good things out of the good stored up in his heart, and an evil man brings evil things out of the evil stored up in his heart. For the mouth speaks what the heart is full of.

So, what spills out you when you're pushed? Tilted over? Well I tell you my biggest reason for walking on the eggshells was because whenever I did or said something wrong and his glass was tilted over what came out was scary and intimidating. If he was speaking out of the abundance of his heart, there was a lot of bitterness, anger and rage and it had been there for a very long time. At the same token I had to watch myself. This goes right back to the beginning of this book where we discussed guarding our hearts. I had to remember what this bible verse was and I had to keep reminding myself to keep praying, keep worshipping and watch what came out my mouth. What came out my mouth would determine what was inside my heart. However, the brokenness, sadness and tiredness was sooner or later going to spill. It took lots of discipline to keep it together but I needed to discipline my thoughts more. Why my thoughts? Because it was my thought process that kept my emotions tied to what people would say, what he would do to me, shame, confusion and bondage.

As each day went by, I just kept trying to tune out the insults. I had a job that didn't pay much and contributed what I had to the house. That wasn't enough, I had to hear that everyday of how it wasn't enough. We weren't the only ones in the household. He had two older kids. One very sweet girl who had been bedridden all her life. Every time I think of her my heart swells with love. She was the hope I saw everyday. She didn't know much but she knew how to praise and she would sometimes connect with my heart. She'll look at me and ask me to sing or dance to worship. Those were my happy moments. In the house, there also was his other daughter who because

of life's harshness became bitter sweet. Didn't trust anyone, thirsty for love, acknowledgment and very possessive of her father, home etc. Each one of his daughters received a check because of their disabilities. He on the other hand didn't work. He claimed he was a full time minister but that was not the case. Yet, he always put down my job and always put down my pay and he never appreciated that I'd give what I had. It was just my income and his daughter's incomes coming in to the home. At home, there were also home attendants that came to work. There was one particular home attendant who at one moment was affirming me and the next was gossiping. He treated her as if she was the lady of the house. From the moment she started working that April 2013 I knew she'd be trouble. Her attire in itself spoke volumes. As a professional, her chest should've not been so exposed and as a professional her sex life with her man should've never been discussed. Every time I tried to point something out or share my discomfort about something he'd burst and call me a fool, or slap me. I started becoming resentful of this lady because here I was the wife and she could do what she wanted with the home and I couldn't say BOO! Before she came there were two other home attendants. Both use to tell me "Miss Genie, please ignore him when he's upset he's a walking time bomb." One of them told me you shouldn't put up with this and she even once cornered me in kitchen because she noticed I was hiding something. It was a busted bottom lip.
He had slapped me because he was angry at one of his ex-wives. At another time, we were on train almost

getting home, when a billboard on train got my attention and he literally yelled at me and slapped my mouth. He yelled: You're disgusting I see you checking out that man!"
What man? I was reading a billboard that had a school on it. Really?
In all of these instances, I didn't fight back. My glass was just getting fuller but I wouldn't let it completely tilt. I ran after him trying to explain myself. Every word had to always be measured. Every thought had to be broken down for him to understand. I knew this was unhealthy, but how do I untie this knot? Wasn't God going to hold me accountable for leaving if I did? And why did I love this man so much but feared him as well? What was wrong with me?

For a long time, I made excuses for his insecurities, though he never admitted being insecure, bitter or angry. But an insecure person will rarely admit it, they will instead show the signs of insecurity and it may show off in the nastiest way possible. If there was one thing I was learning in all this I can admit was patience. But the line had to be drawn somewhere. But when? But how?

My dear friend, you're probably reading this and feeling chills down your spine because you're remembering a time you went through this or you're in this right now. Maybe, you're not abused or been abused but you're a walking time bomb and your mouth overflow is as bad as the sewers in your city. It's time to look at your

heart. Perhaps you're that husband that calls his wife names, or that wife that calls her husband names, that mother who puts down her children, that boss who tears down his employees. Watch your mouth, watch your heart.
If your heart has been left unguarded, then it's been deceived and if it's been deceived it's speaking foolish things every time the launch button is pushed.

Your mouth can heal or break, mend or destroy your personality. Your temper can make a fool out of you. It's time to discipline your mouth, tongue and thoughts.

Philippians 4:8King James Version (KJV) 8 Finally, brethren, whatsoever things are true, whatsoever things are honest, whatsoever things are just, whatsoever things are pure, whatsoever things are lovely, whatsoever things are of good report; if there be any virtue, and if there be any praise, think on these things.

Marriage is built on trust. All relationships are built on trust. Trust is earned, it doesn't violate the other person's feelings. No one should be bound to a relationship where they have to watch whatever they say and be held back from communicating how they feel. Oftentimes, when one cannot communicate with the other because they're afraid of the whips that will flow out the mouth of their spouse they then isolate themselves, grow bitter, depressed and it's a recipe for disaster.

In some instances, the fear and intimidation is so much that some have resorted to suicide.
  According to this article; Female Suicide and Domestic Violence

Domestic violence is a factor in up to one-quarter of female suicide attempts. Female victims of domestic violence have eight times the risk for suicide compared with the general population. Fifty percent of battered women who attempt suicide undertake subsequent attempts. Married females experience lower suicide rates compared with single females. However, if domestic violence is present in the marriage, the risk of suicide increases. If a pregnant woman is a victim of domestic violence, the risk of suicide increases.

Believe me when I tell you I had to fight those thoughts of not living anymore. But thank God for His grace and eternal love. I don't know where you're in your life right now. I don't know if anything I'm saying applies to you or someone you know. One thing I know is no one's breath is to be snuffed out. Suicide is not the answer, you are not bound by your circumstances. Yes, I sense some of you beginning to get clarity, feel a relief and what's that I hear? It's you're heartbeat! Well my darling, it's not over – you are still breathing!
Notes to self:

Chapter 6

Prince turned frog!

One of the many lies we can get caught up in is the "but he has good qualities," They're good things about him. He did so much for me. I got caught in that deceit. Let me explain and pay close attention. I'm the kind of person who likes to give the benefit of the doubt to people, especially after seeing potential, attributes and so forth. It is obvious that the frog wasn't viewed as a frog when we got involved. C'mon now, remember that first look? That first time you spoke? How about that first nice thing he did that blew your mind?

I remember the movie "Enough" starring Jennifer Lopez. Here, she was a waitress and she met a fine looking wealthy man. Everything was total bliss in the beginning, but then he turned out to be abusive and she had to run off. The woman trained and had a face-off with this man. Now ladies, I'm not telling you go watch the movie and then go beat your husband. What I'm saying is that the story line in the movie "Enough" is a real story in many of our lives today. It never starts off bad. If I were to sit here and write he was a turnoff on day one I'm a big liar. I loved everything about this man. I loved everything I perceived as to being real. I loved his looks, loved the fact he was a Christian and very gifted. He had the ability to preach and sing. He was a neat freak, raised two kids on his own. Dressed to impress. He traveled on the train to New Jersey just to see me, he brought me gifts, very practical ones. Was always concerned whether I ate or not, I mean he was almost perfect. Many reached out to me to tell me about his reputation. Many told me he was a woman abuser. I'll never forget the call from an evangelist friend of mine, let's call him JayJay. He could not believe I was in a relationship with this man. He literally cried as he told me Genie, you're my friend and I love you and I'm scared for you. He's going to destroy your life, your ministry and he's going to take you away from all your friends. I don't want to lose you. He's going to isolate you from everyone. Now, I really thought he was overreacting, perhaps because he knows how terrible my last marriage had ended and how that almost destroyed me and my kids. Yet, all I knew then was God Spoke and I didn't doubt he did. I just kept leaving part of that word out.

When we want what we want, we become of selective hearing ladies and gentlemen, so clean out your ears and take heed to what the spirit of the Lord has been telling you. Always remember there is a will of command and God can will something for us but we can break that command.

Job 36:11
"If they hear and serve Him, They will end their days in prosperity And their years in pleasures.

OUCH! Take a look at that verse. If we don't hear and we don't serve him. Hhhmmmmm, I feel like preaching now. Goodness, to serve is to wait. If we don't wait on the Lord. Somebody start shouting right now. Are you with me? If we fail to hear God and wait on Him, we will not end in prosperity but instead emotional, distressful calamity. There's no pleasure in pain.

Let me take you three days before I met this man. First of all, I had him on my social network pages for a few years. However, we never became friends on there. It was just network and I had not paid him any mind except for a few months beforehand, I looked just at his profile picture and felt I knew him in my spirit. I left that alone. One day, I'm walking with a friend of mine and she and I got curious about this church that happened to be opened. To cut the long story short, we went upstairs and from the moment I entered inside the Pastor knew I was a pastor. God began to use him to reveal things that were to come which did come to pass with my church and other areas of my life. But one strange thing was that I had a "true love waits ring" and he told me I had to remove it and put it on my other hand because God was going to reveal who my husband was and he could not see a ring on my finger. Now, I was rushing. I received the word but at that time I lived two hours away in New Jersey and had to leave. When I tried to leave he said to me God's not done speaking. As I approached the door, I literally fell on my rear. He continued to say, I told you God wasn't done. In three days, you will meet him. He's been through many things, he must heal. You will

know who he is, you will feel it in your spirit. But you are to not rush at all. He must be processed.
Two days later, I'm asked at last minute to MC a concert. Day three, yes here I was, had totally forgotten about that word until I had to present this next singer myself.

What am I saying? We need to hear God and wait on him. Some things fail not because God didn't speak, but because we didn't follow instructions and adhere to shortcuts instead.
Read your bible extensively, you'll see God gave Noah specific instructions, God gave Moses specific instructions, on and on you'll see God always gave instructions.
The victory is found in following instructions! But when we're needy, lonely, just feeding into our fleshly urges and desires we tend to listen partially. This is why many marriages today end in divorce, not hearing, waiting and following instructions. This is why many lose careers, dreams, etc.

No, me not following instructions did not give him a right to abuse me. But it made me chase after a prince who was gonna turn into a frog. I looked at his princely image and didn't think on anything else. Same happens with men. Some of you know "That girl is poison" but you want what you want and that skirt looks mighty nice on her. Somebody stop me!
Now, when this happens and you wind up oftentimes it involves you going back and reminiscing; I remember when he made me breakfast in bed, I

remember when we preached together and the fire of God came down. Trust me, I thought of all those moments too and I was so eager to see that man I fell head over heels for again that I converted myself into a floor mat, hoping that he would see my humility and come to his senses. But no that wasn't the case, it wasn't that he wasn't the one but it wasn't the time, or maybe he wasn't, I don't even dwell on that anymore, I just know I was blind but now I see and you can't keep making excuses just because he paid your rent sister!

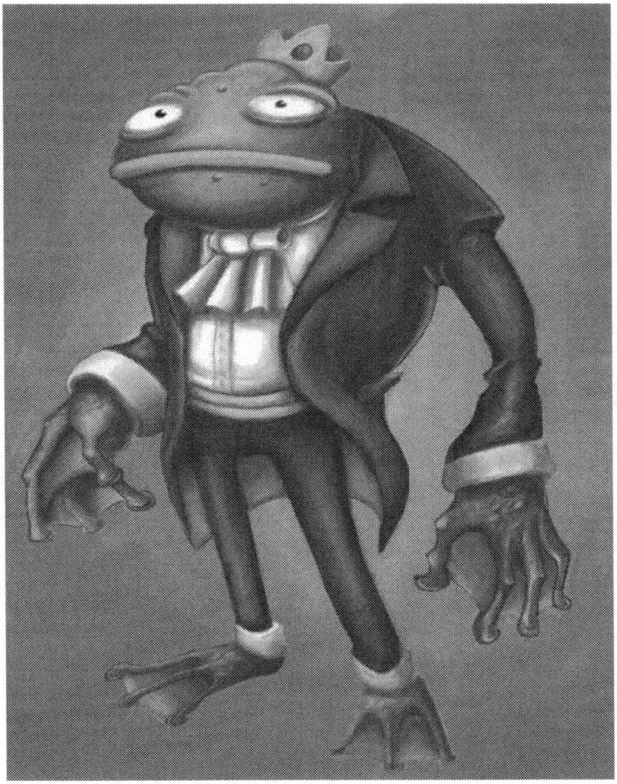

Notes :

Do you know anyone going through abuse right now? What can you do to help?

_____

_____
_____

Chapter 7
To love or to detox?

Break free of toxic people and relationships, they erode your quality of life.

Ty Howard

When a woman is in love she can sometimes make so many excuses for that toxic boyfriend, husband etc. Especially, if she's confused and surrounded by people in the religious circuit that tell her she can't break free because it's a sin. I'll tell you what sin is. A sin is to allow someone have so much power over you that he would destroy the very thing that is the apple of God's eye, YOU! Now, let's take a look at God's word.
Jeremiah 29:11 Amplified Bible (AMP)

11 For I know the plans and thoughts that I have for you,' says the Lord, 'plans for peace and well-being and not for disaster, to give you a future and a hope.

Dear reader you may be making excuses for this person in your life because you're afraid to walk away and or maybe you are receiving advice to put up with abuse . Perhaps someone is telling you this is long suffering and what God expects for you to do in this unhealthy marriage . Let me take a moment to break this down .

First thing first God's plans for you are of peace. Is this relationship bringing any peace to you?
If you're about to tie the knot, perhaps you fell into passion before time and you're being told it's the right thing to do, meanwhile you have red flags going up on all directions, don't go further.

The right thing to do is look at God's word and get out of that relationship before you tie the knot. God's plans are of peace, now check this, His plans are not of disaster, instead they're for your well being. Do you really think dear reader that God's plan was for you to get married and endure abuse from him /her and the family too? Would God tell you to stay in something that can be disastrous for your life? Just like you, I didn't want to hear it. My heart and mind was set. I loved him unconditionally and I stood there being a living sacrifice because of excuses I made up for him. Jesus had already died for him, if he didn't want to live to God's full potential and wanted to trample on the blood that was on him. But I stood, I believed God and I'm not going to lie, I experienced God and his mercy through this like never seen before in my life. God knew my heart and used this unto his glory, yet, I don't believe he was pleased with me staying in that place of hurt, but he loved me through it and eventually saw me out of it.

The moment I let him get away with the first smack, the second, the insults, I opened up a can of worms. I allowed him the space to abuse me. Somehow, in my heart I wanted to change him with my unconditional love but didn't realize that God's love did not include me being a martyr for him. I remember one Thursday evening, early July 2013, on our bed time to wind down and go to sleep. We always had these moments of peace but it was never permanent. I remember we played cards, watched movies but this night he was in a strange mood. He was in one of those moods where I had to turn on the eggshells alert. I was laying down, the TV was on and he was lying next to me. No prior arguments, everything was cool. Then he asked me this

question "Has anyone ever despised you?" I looked at him and said what? No, no one has despised me and he responded "Well, I despise you." My heart was raising, my thoughts were raising, and I said to myself this is going to start something. I was annoyed, he kept on saying things to me and cursing me with obscene language and I couldn't stay shut anymore. I finally responded "babe, I bought Scope, it's in the bathroom use some. How could you speak that way when you're preaching tomorrow night?" That was like igniting hell's flames, he began to smack my face uncontrollably, I had to fight to get him off me and he picked up a pillow to suffocate me and that's when I used all my strength and nails to push him off. And I was screaming from the pain, he finally came to his senses and cried. He threw himself on his knees and asked God to forgive him, meanwhile, I couldn't close my mouth because I thought he had broken my jaw. He began to cry and say he was sorry and I tried to move my mouth to beg for help. He said "Genie, I'm sorry please don't call 911 if you do they will take my daughter (who was bedbound) away from me. You love her, you don't want her to go to a foster home." I was in great pain that I even began to vomit.
He went crazy, then said he was going to run away and leave me with his daughters, then he was opening window on the 9th floor to jump out and I had to in my excruciating pain stop him. He tried running out door, I stopped him. I could barely talk as I laid in bed put on a preaching and thought to myself, what am I doing here? He kept apologizing, calmed down and laid next to me promising he will never do it again. His

bedbound daughter meant so much to me and I allowed my feelings to manipulate me and betray me. Not realizing that the worst was yet to come. Who can I turn to? I was too embarrassed to tell anyone. The next morning, his other daughter called me from her room mocking and laughing saying "Papi (daddy) gave you a beating last night huh. You're not the first or the last" and she then hung up the phone . That night with a slightly swelled face and my hair mane covering it, I went with him to the service he was preaching at. I was on my knees praying when he grabbed my hands and kissed them saying I was the most compassionate woman and thanked me for forgiving him. I remember he couldn't get through his song without breaking down and after preaching he asked me to come up to the front and spoke wonders of me and begged for prayers for our marriage. Was he sincere? Was it a show? I couldn't tell, I couldn't feel, I couldn't think right...

What excuses are you making? I should've seen there was no future and hope was dim if I continued to tolerate this. What are you tolerating? Do you really think that you can stay in this and not suffer the worst? God can restore, but both parties have to allow that restoration in their individual lives first.

I'd like to direct myself at you beginning a relationship, seeing red flags and staying in it. What excuses are you making?

Here are some excuses I found in an article written by

Jenn Chan for "Elite Daily"
"He's a great Guy; 7 Excuses Women Consistently Make For Their Horrible Boyfriends
1. He will change.
Whether the guy is a couch potato or a big flirt, the excuse you incessantly make for him is that "he'll change."
2. We are not official.
This excuse is for the guy's flirtatious behavior.

You know that he's messaging or possibly even hooking up with other girls, but technically you two aren't officially together yet.
Therefore, you excuse his behavior because you don't want to come off as a needy or clingy person.
3. I know he cares.
"Deep down in his heart he really cares for me." Or not. If a guy really cares, he will show it.
4. He won't do it again.
He may have cheated, abused you (physically or verbally), or thrown your sh*t out, but because he apologized, you give him the benefit of the doubt that it won't happen again.
5. He's busy.
He doesn't respond to your messages as often as you'd hope. You only get to see him once a week and your friends start to ask you, "Oh, where's X?" The most justifiable answer is, "He's busy with work/school."
6. He messages and sees me as much as he can.
Similar to excuse number five, we'd like to believe that you reply and see us as much as you can.
Even though we know you read the message, we'd like to think that you couldn't reply right away because you were busy with work.
7. He's not ready for a relationship.
Whether he's still getting over his ex or enjoying the single life, he's just not ready (although some of the things you guys do together suggest otherwise).
You don't want to push him into a corner, nor do you want to be that girl to suffocate him. Therefore, you excuse his unfaithfulness or lack of commitment by suggesting that, "He's not ready."

Girls don't like to argue with the people they like and care about. Sometimes, making excuses for the guy we like is much easier than admitting to reality. It prevents heated debates that will most likely end up nowhere. We also make excuses for the guy we like because we don't want to be humiliated. No girl wants to feel like an idiot, and making excuses is one of many defense mechanisms to prevent ourselves from feeling hurt or embarrassed.

What's the number one reason we make excuses? Duh! We like you! It's as simple as that. However, we have to realize that if the guy is a repeat offender, then it is definitely not okay. It's best to take a step back and reevaluate the situation.

A healthy relationship does not include making excuses.

So, now I direct myself to the abused and torn hearts, to the leaders that either sweep these situations underneath a rug or force a woman to stay in an abused state of mind because God hates divorce. Have you stopped to think, does he hate abuse too? That abuse is infidelity as well?

When do we as leaders or we as the abused say enough is enough?

Here's some thoughts written by Gary Thomas, Enough Is Enough

Enough is enough!

Jesus says there are "levels" of love, and times when one loyalty must rise over another. Our loyalty to marriage is good and noble and true. But when loyalty to a relational structure allows evil to continue it is a false loyalty, even an evil loyalty.

Christian leaders and friends, we have to see that some evil men are using their wives' Christian guilt and our teaching about the sanctity of marriage as a weapon to keep harming them. I can't help feeling that if more women started saying, "This is over" and were backed up by a church that enabled them to escape instead of enabling the abuse to continue, other men in the church tempted toward the same behavior might finally wake up and change their ways.

Christians are more likely to have one-income families, making some Christian wives feel even more vulnerable. We have got to clean up our own house. We have got to say "Enough is enough." We have got to put the fear of God in some terrible husbands' hearts, because they sure don't fear their wives and their lack of respect is leading to an ongoing deplorable behavior.

I want a man who was abusive to have to explain to a potential second wife why his saintly first wife left him. Let men realize that behavior has consequences, and that wives are supposed to be cherished and not to be used, not abused, and never treated as sexual playthings. If a man wants the benefit and companionship of a good woman let him earn it and re-earn it, and let him know it can be lost.

Enough is enough.

Great thoughts Gary Thomas has on this subject right? So I now ask, has your enough just arrived? So do you continue to love and stay? Or should you begin to detox from that toxic relationship. I say get ready to breath again.

Have you ever felt like enough is enough ?
What actions did you take or not take?

_____

Chapter 8

When is Enough, Enough?

"so far as you continue to entertain what makes you unhappy, you shall always dance to the tune of what will make you unhappy. A mindset change can cause a great change."
— Ernest Agyemang Yeboah

I look back at times and ask myself, how did you do it? What kept you there? When was enough, enough? I'm sure this was also the question for many who did want me to run the other direction away from this man. If I were to write every single detail of what I went through in the pages of this book, I think I'd never be done writing. My goal focus here is to help you who are in the beginning stages of an abusive, red flag alert relationship to walk away now. I also pray and hope I can build the courage of you who is being abused and if you the abuser is also reading this, my prayer is that you would admit you have a problem and you need to get professional and spiritual help. I also pray that I can reach those pastors and other folks who really believe and teach that a woman must submit and stay under oppressive and abusive circumstances. I had all kinds of voices speaking, from those who said stay and fight, avoid a divorce and to those who would say run! My emotions, I must admit were like a pretzel at the time. My heart was just shattered and my dreams felt violated. I, however was passionate about making it work and passionate about helping him heal, losing myself in that process. Let me take this back to one of the first red flags I saw. Please read this carefully because I want you to understand that red flags cannot be ignored. When there's a red flag, that's a siren going off. Yes, people are imperfect but you cannot allow your fear of loss, acceptance, ridicule, rejection and loneliness keep you in a place that's gonna set you up for great heartache! There was one evening I visited him at his place and his child's home attendant had cooked. I remember he set up the table. I tell you, this man did everything to impress me in the beginning. But he out of nowhere took his fork and slammed it against the wall. I froze, I said to myself this isn't good but I stood still. He then said "I'm sorry baby" and began to just burst about his youngest daughter's mom whom he had divorced a few years prior to meeting me. Apparently, she wouldn't let him see his daughter because of him being seen with me. I gave him words of encouragement and I excused it. This led to other little incidents, and then to the bigger ones and they just escalated and escalated to the point where truly I can say God kept me. In God's mercy, because he knew the intentions of my heart, even though I stood when I should've left and trusted him, he looked upon me with love, grace and mercy. But dear, make no mistakes there are some women who stay and I'm sure God nudged them to leave but they stood and they're not alive to tell the story. So, please you're not reading this by accident, God is telling you let go. I've created you, you're mine. I didn't design you to be a floor mat. Whether it's physical, verbal, mental, emotional and spiritual abuse it's all unacceptable. I knew these things were unacceptable, but every time I turned to some preacher from overseas or someone I didn't know would literally drop a word. Would tell me prophetically my marriage will be restored, my husband will return, he will change etc. Now I'm not going to say it wasn't God, I'm very careful with that, but then again why would God keep me in such pain? If you feel God is speaking to you, I can tell you this, walk away from the problem. If God can transform later on and restore amen. But while this man or even women is hitting you, torturing you, endangering you – Don't stay in it. God don't need you there for him to work. I now understand that very clearly.

Very rare will an abuser change. Though, personally in my family and with good friends I've seen men turned around in such a way that left me speechless. Transformation is available through the power of Jesus Christ, but the individual must want to be transformed and delivered and also get professional help. Even then, you must wait a long time to see the good fruit bear. . Some abusers pretend to change just so they can get their foot in to control you again. Besides lots of prayer and fasting at the time, I did try to address some of his issues, because I was aware of his childhood abuse, history and background of a rough upbringing. Again, remember I was playing hero, so even after the beatings, a set up that led me to be locked up for 14 hours made homeless, yet I forgave him. Yes, I found myself putting up with him showing up at work, seeking me out and me giving in to him. It didn't matter to him if I was pregnant, homeless, he continued to neglect me, control me, abuse me mentally and so forth. Throughout all these mentioned times, I tried finding solutions to his problems not seeing I had a bigger problem, bigger than criticism, bigger than the gossip from his circle, bigger than his slaps —MY DECEIVED HEART!

So when enough was enough instead of leaving him, I encouraged him to go for mental health care. I made him an appointment for intake at THE BLANTON-PEALE COUNSELING CENTER in NYC. I went with him a few times for support and he hated it when the therapist assigned to him asked certain questions. He started missing appointments, complained about the Therapist and about the travel time to the city, so I searched another route. I then set up another intake appointment at The Fordham Mental Health Center in the Bronx and again I'd meet up with him (this is after living separately) and I would go accompany him to his appointments. He would then tell me he purposely would say things that didn't make sense for fun. He eventually stopped attending and wasn't willing to receive whatever diagnose they were giving him. He said to me they canceled appointments, had me call them and I was told he kept missing his appointments.

So when was enough, enough Genie? After infidelity scandals? No, I refused to give up on him, held on. I started feeling guilty if I quit Him. He insulted me through various emails and hours later would pop out at my place to be with me in many levels, he would leave and this repeated itself over and over. There were times we sat by the water at a favorite park and he would tell me, why do I need a therapist? I have you, I can just do with you what I do with her, Talk! He'd say things like how he wanted to sometimes stop living and he'd share scary thoughts of how he battled with killing people in his mind but was too old to go to jail. He'd share and express his unforgiveness toward others. In all this I fought guilt. Guilt? Yes, I felt if something happens to him it's because one more person gave up on him. I envisioned him healed, set free, and delivered. Ministering with power and anointing, full of God's love. But again, clearly all this was deceit. My heart deceived me, I didn't guard it.

Dear reader, God does not call us to fix people! We are to love, encourage, admonish, instruct, but if there is someone that is hurting you, deceiving you, taking advantage of you, abusing you, endangering you, please don't stay!

Love from a distance, love yourself first. Draw a line in the sand and declare enough is enough!

I'd like to conclude this chapter with some thoughts from Mack Lamouse he wrote in an article "When Enough Is Enough" –How to End an Abusive Relationship.

The question of when you should get out of an abusive relationship is one that can be answered simply - you should get out of a relationship as soon as possible. Abusive relationships, whether emotionally abusive or physically abusive are bad for your well-being and health and often dangerous. Even if the abuse is 'only' psychological to begin with, it often progresses into physical abuse later on and can still place a large amount of stress on the abused party and even lead to depression. In a physically abusive relationship, however it can be far more dangerous early on, and even if the abuser does not intend to cause serious damage it can still end in death or broken limbs if they lose their temper or misjudge a punch. Once you are in an abusive relationship it becomes incredibly difficult to escape (particularly if you are afraid of your partner or they've primed you to become dependent on them) and the longer it continues the harder it will become. For these reasons, you should get out as soon as possible, no matter the nature of the abuse, and if you cannot do it yourself you should get help.

So my friend, there it goes. Don't stay ... That first flag should be enough to not see him again. What God has for you will not cause you pain. But hey, I'm not done yet, the next chapters reveal many things untold to understand my views, more about my painful journey, the deceit I believed in, the things that caused me brokenness and how God delivered me. .

Notes to self :

Chapter 9

Wrinkled Table Placemats

"One's dignity may be assaulted, vandalized and cruelly mocked, but it can never be taken away unless it is surrendered."
— Michael J. Fox

Spot cleaning is a cleaning method that concentrates solely on cleaning specific areas of the garment. "Spot Clean Only" means that there is no safe way of cleaning the entire garment in a commercial cleaning machine. Damage to the garment may result if put through the professional dry cleaning process. – Cudneys.com

Saturday morning arrived, I had survived a strange week. I had been walking on eggshells and felt so mentally worn out with everything going on in my relationship with my husband, his daughter and his circle. When I mentioned his circle, I am speaking of certain people who remained close to him, exes included that had an outside influence on his decisions in our marriage or on his thinking. His main priority was to keep his image clean and redeem himself from his past reputation. That implied using who he had to use and doing what he had to do at all cost because his claim was that he had always been the used and abused one.

That whole week he continued mentioning how I had to find a place to go to because his family was coming in from Puerto Rico and Boston. I remember looking at him as if he had three heads. First, I was his wife, I slept on his bed. Secondly, we were living in a three bedroom apartment with enough space and a futon couch in the living room. Thirdly, he never had anything really nice to say about his family. He kept in touch because he felt they owed him. He was given up for adoption and reconnected with his biological family in his late adulthood, not too many years prior and now all of a sudden they're coming and I have to leave. Well, getting back to Saturday morning, I remember sitting on the dining room table to drink some coffee, when I saw that the placemats were very wrinkled and out of shape. I'm very particular with things and I had planned to spot clean them because that's what the label said, but being that I worked five days a week, I planned to get to them that weekend. So, I questioned; what happened to the placemats honey? That was like the question from hell.

Not that the question was wrong, but it was just what he was waiting for to initiate conflict and he took advantage of it.

Immediately, he began to yell. He shouted how ungrateful I was. How the home attendant who we call Teresita washed the placemats as a favor. He calls her out and tells her what a disgrace of a woman I was. I simply went toward her and said, I understand you tried helping and thank you. The placemats had a tag that said spot clean that's why I had not thrown them in laundry. Anytime you decide to do something, if you're not sure please feel free to ask me. She said ok because she didn't know how to read English, I said fine just ask and thanks. No big deal to me but it became a big deal to him. He needed a reason to have me leave the house. He was trying from the 4th day of marriage. Now that's another chapter. A few moments later, he comes out shouting from the back room calling me all names. Telling me I had to leave, Teresita had lied about me and told him I was accusing her of having something with him. I couldn't believe she was even crying. Acting at its best. I approached her and said I've never accused you of such thing, I've just asked you to stop sharing with my husband about your love of watching pornography with your man and to wear a more appropriate shirt within the house. She was a very busty lady and wasn't ever wearing her scrubs or something more modest for work. This escalated to a shouting match where he walked away to living room shouting and continued to do so and I had had it and shouted back "This behavior of yours is what's pushed many people away from you." "You have a problem and you shouldn't be bringing in anyone into our marriage issues." Now one his daughters, Celine begins to shout as well from her room. Calling me a female dog and telling me to leave her father F******* alone.

I remember the feelings of feeling bullied, tired, isolated from everyone and just didn't know what or how to continue handling this, but within me, I had not mustered the courage to get out of it.

I stood in front her door and said to Celine, "Celine, this is between your dad and I. Honey please I'm going to ask you to stay out of it." At this time, he walks by into our room which was directly across. She continued to curse me and now I said to her "Don't act like you're protecting your father after we know and have the evidence that you called Adult Protective Services, stating he was sexually abusing you and financially exploiting you."

Yes, that was probably not what I should've done. In the heat of the moment even when truth is told you might start a war and at this point out to this young lady who had abandonment issues, rejection issues, anger, hate, hurts and felt like I was her rival was just ignited to attack at a whole other level.

I had already experienced her morning visits to the room when her dad would step out to take his other daughter to her bus. I had already been bullied, threatened, mocked and I kept it all quiet to maintain maximum peace, just so he would not beat her, for they both had many encounters.

But at this time, I just couldn't stay quiet anymore. Celine in anger cursed me out and told me to get the f**** out her house.

Knowing that what I said was true, he said to me you should've never said that to her. Now, you heard her get out and he took one of my purses and threw it emptying its contents on floor.

I remember going in and saying to him you know I have nowhere to go and you know I've done nothing wrong. He said he was going to call police if I didn't leave. In my stupidity, I replied back. Sometimes, we can tend to give in to someone else's nonsense and create a bigger problem. That was the scenario here. We must learn to keep our emotions intact and keep silent in the heat of the moment. Then think and get out of the situation.

My reply was "I've been living here for three months, I'm married to you. After a person has lived over thirty days you can't just throw them out. Why have you been trying to throw me out, why did you even marry me? I am not going anywhere. I went and got on my knees and began to pray.

He said when I get back you better be gone. I just continued to pray.

He left and then she left too and the only ones in the home was his bedridden daughter and Teresita. I remember feeling so anxious, so scared. Finally, picked up the phone and called the pastor who we had been sitting under for three months. I called to share my struggle, he bluntly asked me what was going on and I spoke the truth. I admitted to the abuse. I was embarrassed but had no choice. However, I was given instructions to stay cool, quiet and collective. We would sit down after church Sunday.

I stood in the bedroom all day. I remember just talking to God and too ashamed to tell anyone what was going on. Depression began to sink in and thoughts of ending my life began to encircle me. I cried and cried so much. He kept the medications he took on his night stand and I took one bottle and poured the pills in my hands. I laid on the floor by the window – I cried and cried and battled for my life. I told God I was tired of the whole situation, I told God this didn't make sense at all, I told God if he was the one he wouldn't mistreat me. I'm ashamed, my family is angry at me for marrying him, friends have walked away and those that remain I can't get in touch with. He had threatened me so many times of breaking my mouth if I told anyone our business.

So here I laid, wanting to end it all, but there was a real fear arising in my spirit, the fear of being separated from God if I chose to end my own life. The pain I'd cause my children. The joy I'd cause my enemies. So as I put pills back in bottle while still sobbing, I heard Teresita call my name from behind the door.

Truly, I thought to myself what does this woman want from me after her drama, her lies and siding with my husband. She comes in and says "Genie, get up oh My God." Genie I hope you're not thinking of hurting yourself. I'm sorry about everything that's happened. You haven't eaten all day. You must eat. I said no I don't want to eat. She said I'm making a flan so you can have some. Stop crying you're going to get sick. The look on my face must've been priceless for the confusion to set in. Why is she caring now? A little while later, I heard my husband come in and ask her, did she leave already? I heard her telling him no, she's not well. Check up on her. Don't fight anymore and his response was I don't care. I want her out. He gave her instructions to take his daughter out and she said I don't think Genie should be left alone. He said "I don't care." Evening was closing in, she had left for a bit and he never came to the room, he also left. I didn't know who to call and my question was where should I go? What will people say? We're newlyweds. I love him but why doesn't he love me? Or does he? I was such an emotional broken mess. A call came in it was my other stepdaughter one who lived out of state. This young lady didn't grow up with him. She had a different mindset, very nice to me. She called to warned me and show me how her sister Celine was out on the town with one of his exes. I believe his daughter had the same questions I had. If this woman supposedly tried destroying him, closed up many doors and he spoke of her as the worst thing that happened to him, then why is his daughter with her? His daughter from out of town asked me to stay calm, don't argue with him, and pay no mind to Celine again as I was told to keep my cool, just be quiet when he gets back.

Teresita got back with Annie and out her in bed. She had cut a piece of flan and came to me saying you must try to eat something. I sat and ate it and stood quiet. I went back to the room, sat on our bed and thought of all his daughter Celine had told me. I thought on how I wasn't the first woman on that bed, how unfaithful he was and how he tried choking the previous wife in the closet. I questioned myself on why did I marry him? I knew he had been under a restraining order that kept him from a younger child. I knew he had 8 kids from different moms, it couldn't have been they were all evil. The only kids he took care of was the two that lived with him and on and off the younger one. But why was he so distant from the others? What did these women really do? And all the ex-girlfriends, mainly all women in some position in church. How could it be that he was their victim? All these thoughts raced through my head. Then, I began to get texts stating he was seen in a van with another woman. Why was I constant being mocked? Harassed?

He came back and ordered Teresita to go home and told her I'd watch Annie. He left and Teresita asked me to keep an eye on my stepdaughter Annie. Annie always knew when I was sad, Annie was special and another reason I didn't want to leave. I loved her. Hours went by and finally Celine gets home with the wife of a friend of theirs , who was a cop. Yes she escorted her to the door. I smelled something wasn't right. She had been out with one of her fathers exes and now she's walked to the door by this cop friend. The cop friend says "hey Genie how are you?" Randomly hugs me. Seen her countless of times, never hugged me before. I was polite and then I went to my room. The texts from some unrecognized number continued saying cruel things to me. I knocked on Celine's door and asked her where her father is? (I should've never even bothered doing that. But when your emotions are disarrayed you don't think) she responded to stay the f*** away from her. So I went back to my room.
It was after midnight around 12:30am when he got home. I didn't stay quiet as I had been advised. I was tired of being quiet. I asked him where was he and who he was with and showed him the texts. He ignored me,

I could smell beer on him. I questioned, he had a liver problem and I was surprised to smell anything on him, according to him he quit drinking long ago. He walked over to his dresser and removes his watch, gets his pjs and goes for a shower.

When he returned to the room he was sarcastic and said he didn't want to hear anything I had to say. I sat on the bed with tears streaming down my face. I didn't know how to be quiet and in a very monotone voice, I began to share how unhappy I felt. How horrible it was to get married, put my things in a storage and leave clothes in a hamper. Five closets in the home and my clothes in a hamper, only seasonal clothes everything else was in storage. How unhappy I was that I was the Mrs. but decisions of the household were made by him and the home attendants. I couldn't even add a nail to the wall. Why did he allow his daughter and home attendants to come into our marriage and circumstances we're faced with? I expressed I loved him but it was so empty. How tired I was of not being able to connect with my friends because he'd cut short my calls and shut off the TV on me if I began texting. I should've just gone to sleep. I should've, could've, and would've…..

I did not foresee what was up next. Dear reader, you who are experiencing the abuse. The abuser will never hear you out with his heart. He will hear you out with his selfish agenda. Being quiet and moving strategically out of the situation is the safest thing. When I say quiet I'm not saying don't tell others what you're going through, I'm saying don't talk back to the abuser, nor try to explain anything. It just may be the biggest setup for your destruction.

In the pages to come you'll see what I mean. But for now let's take a look at some facts about abuse. According to Darlene Lancers blog on www.psychologytoday.com.

Facts about Abuse

Victims often minimize violence. This is their denial. Violence includes throwing or breaking things, slapping, shoving, hair-pulling, and forced sex. Here are some facts you should know:

Usually, abuse takes place behind closed doors.
Abusers deny their actions.
Abusers blame the victim.
Violence is preceded by verbal abuse.
Abuse damages your self-esteem.
The abuser needs to be right and in control.
The abuser is possessive and may try to isolate their partner from friends and family.
The abuser is hypersensitive and may react with rage.
A gun in the house increases the risk of homicide by 500 percent.
Two-thirds of domestic violence perpetrators have been drinking.
One-third of victims have been drinking or using drugs.

Before we continue I'd like to say that if you need to

speak to someone and you must get out, don't wait until you finish reading this book, or until something worst escalates.
Here are a few numbers you can call.

The National Domestic Violence Hotline
1-800-799-7233

For domestic violence victims:
800-621-HOPE (4673)

XtrememeasuresNYC:
xtrememeasureactivist@gmail.com

"... you don't have to wait for someone to treat you bad repeatedly. All it takes is once, and if they get away with it that once, if they know they can treat you like that, then it sets the pattern for the future."
— Jane Green, Bookends

Chapter 10
How far could he go to create an alibi?

"All too often women believe it is a sign of commitment, an expression of love, to endure unkindness or cruelty, to forgive and forget. In actuality, when we love rightly we know that the healthy, loving response to cruelty and abuse is putting ourselves out of harm's way."
— bell hooks, All About Love

So, here I was with tears streaming down my face, calmly expressing how I truly felt in hopes he would hear me with his heart. But instead he turned off the lights and I sat there on the bed while he laid down just sharing my disappointment. I guess I was hoping it makes sense to him and he'd realize how horrible he was treating me. I guess I thought he'd say he was sorry, hug me and promise he'd never make me feel hurt again. But instead, I noticed a little red light beaming from his nightstand. I asked what is that red light? He replied: "I'm recording you so you can hear how stupid you sound."
I said OK! Good, you can then rewind and listen to me again. You never listened.
At this point he said, "if you don't shut up I'm going to call the police right away." Then, he randomly got up said he was calling the police to get me out of his house that he was tired of me. I said no, don't do that there's no reason to call the police. I remember he

turned on the light and began to yell out "Celine call the police, Genie slapped me."
I had not slapped him, I was just talking to him. I just wanted to be heard. My anxiety levels rocketed, I didn't know how to stop him and I pleaded with him not involve his daughter in this. Keep her out!

Before I go on, let me share a little insight about his daughter and my relationship with her. Celine though having to use a walker to walk was otherwise very vivid, outgoing young lady. She'd party a lot, ran away from home with a boyfriend at one time, was in and out of relationships that hurt her severely. She pretty much lived the life of a rebellious young girl. She argue, she'd curse anyone out and she like her father had the other side of her that make people including myself at one time feel sorry for her. From day one, he told me he did not want me to get close to her for she ruined every relationship he had. When we first got engaged, we went straight to where she was at. Celine had gotten a leg surgery at that time so she can straighten them out and walk without the assistance of a walker. I use to visit, helped sponge bathe her since she refused to let the nurses do it and requested I did. I found that as a huge task and test being that she hated me yet needed my help, I humbled myself and was there for her putting aside her previous insults and offenses toward me. I encouraged her, drew faces on her toes to make her laugh. I tried so hard to be a mother, a friend but nothing worked no matter how hard I tried. The abandonment of her mother at 9months and being raised by a man who had women

come in and out of her life I guess made her very angry and so now she was very angry at the fact that he got engaged to me and when I showed her the ring she said; this is gold and diamonds, I thought you had no money. I think she thought he'd use her benefits money being that he didn't work and it was his daughter's checks that paid the bills in their home at the time. But in actuality he used money owed to him that he received and even still she was angry. In the beginning, before things got crazy, he would enjoy buying me shoes, surprising me, taking me to do my hair and he'd tell me not to tell his daughter that he did such things. I had to hide everything he did for me or gave me from her and he did not want me to be close to her.
He went as far as telling me not to lend her my hairbrushes for he wasn't sure if she was meddling in witchcraft.

One morning, she said to me "I'm glad you miscarried, I was afraid as I thought I was going to be replaced." This was coming out of a twenty-year-olds mouth. I was shocked. This young lady wanted me out of that house. We even got married in secret because he was afraid of her and others knowing will lead to sabotaging, not to mention we had premarital intimacy and he was concerned about the pregnancy. One of the home attendants prior to quitting told me Mrs. Genie, Celine is going to do all she can to get rid of you. Be very careful.
 As I mentioned earlier, she'd taunt me in the mornings, tell me all sorts of things about him and

every woman and how he didn't love me. So, here we are now, months later, he's yelling Celine, Genie slapped me, opens the door runs to her across and guess what I did. I went right after him. I tried pulling him by his arm, crying begging him to stop and don't do this to me. By now it was around 2 am. She was sitting with her legs dangling from her full size bed. With her cell in her hand, she looked like that was the cue he'd yelled, looked planned. She said Papi now? I said Celine no please. Why would you call the police on me? I remember pleading with her and reminding her how much stress I'd been through since one of my sons had gotten hit by a car two weeks prior. I just couldn't take any more pain. He had the recorder in his hand and I kept crying and pleading he'd stop doing this and she shouldn't call cops and lie about me. I didn't stop to think Genie if you're calm and walk away there's nothing they can do and they're provoking you. No, I thought oh my God, they're gonna throw me in the street, they're gonna lie to cops, etc.
I thought my heart was going to come out my mouth , my blood pressure felt like was shooting through the sky and here I am begging them to stop for something I never did, he kept yelling Celine call the police, let's get her out of here. As I pulled him out the room, he pushed me, slapped me and I was crying, confused and yelling please stop to them both. At one point he yelled "Oh my heart" Celine she's killing me and threw himself in the hallway floor pretending. She begins to scream and panic in her room. I knew he was faking, I said you have a liver problem, not a heart problem and I moved his leg out the way with my foot, bent over to

grab the recorder. He then quickly grabbed me, pulled me down, got up with his hands around my ankles and dragged me on the floor through the long hallway, back and forth. I was screaming for help, I seriously thought this is it. He's gonna kill me. They're plotting my death. I kept trying to kick him off meanwhile he's yelling Celine call the cops! Somehow, now I see she was hesitant of calling, perhaps deep inside she knew it was wrong but she still gave in to her father's manipulative ways.

Eventually, I was able to escape his grip as I kicked my way off. Now I got up went back into Celine's room to stop her from calling and lying about me. (What I should've done was go to my room and call 911, but my pain wanted to fix things differently). So as I went in, he grabbed me and the wrestling continued, he was hitting me, she was watching, she was laughing, she was shouting it's good for her, among other things and asking when should she call? Obviously, he had been telling her to call but she wasn't dialing yet. Not sure at this point why? Why was she being hesitant? Or was she enjoying the show? He pushed me on the floor and put his body on me, stretches my arms up above my head, I'm screaming for help hoping a neighbor would call 911, he tells her quick Celine I'm restraining her, call now. But everything within me burst with anger. I was under so much duress. I fought back, I was able to reach and bite his arm and as he let go I scratched with the other and got Him off me. This took place right at the foot of her bed and I got up, he grabbed me again by one arm. The breaking point came and I slapped him three times with one hand as hard as I could, shook him off and since she was sitting with her feet dangling from bed when she saw I slapped him she mushed my face, called me a low life, whore and every word imaginable and Frantic with all going on and now her hands are also on me, I slapped her!

I pushed him and ran to my room. Called one of my spiritual daughters. Quicker than I can say peanut butter the cops were there. Their story was that I was violent and I had mental illness and they wanted me to leave. My bruises were not yet showing but since he had a bite mark and scratches, they took his story. However, the cops only said to me,

They don't want you here. Do you have a place to go? I didn't. Not at almost 4 am. So, they told me to sleep in living room, stay to yourself and leave early in the morning. If we get another call, you will both get arrested. I said fine. I got back on the phone with my spiritual daughter. When all of a sudden cops return to the house. They apparently called 911 again! Now, I get these female cops who called me female dog, piece of Sh*** and then came the paramedics to supposedly evaluate me, because I was supposedly mentally ill. Off course, I wasn't mentally ill and so now these cops were bullies. They didn't read me my rights. They just told me change my clothes, leave my cell and just take some money. I was under arrest. Under arrest? For what? Getting abused and defending myself? The allegations had nothing to do with what even happened. The story was that I attacked him and refused to leave. Now, I'm freaking out, why would they go this far? Why did he do this? What person in their right mind would set someone up? It gets better, they arrested me not him. In a domestic violence case here in NY, both get taken in. The original cops that were there beforehand came back. They seemed confused, one of them asked me to relax. He told the female cop, he got me. She said you want to spend the night with this female dog? You could have this garbage. He told her it was unnecessary to say that. He looked at me with compassion, he even took my gown from the bed and asked me if it was mine and wrapped it around my handcuffs. In my whole entire life, I've never had a problem with the law. Here I am married three months later and the hate in these calloused hearts brought them to this. I looked at him and his daughter crying asking them why? Why are you doing this? Why are you lying? I looked at them as I was leaving with the police. There was the cop neighbor right in the living room, same one that walked Celine to the door.

I was taken in, but God's grace never left me. It actually became an amazing experience and testimony. Before I go on, let me mention a few things here. When he's shared this story and when she's shared this story they have portrayed me as this crazy woman who came in and abused them. The whole truth has never been told by them. He vowed after his last ex-wife who did have a restraining order left his house bare when she got fed up with the abuse that he'd never let another woman do that to him. He knew he was abusing me, he knew that his ex-wife and an ex-girlfriend had closed ministerial doors in past and well he had to redeem himself. He always questioned why and how I kept a good testimony. Going back three days before the incident I remember his daughter Celine saying to me, I keep hearing you have a good testimony and many love you. So you're untouchable, I wonder, how untouchable are you? I replied, I'm not perfect, I've had my flaws but I try to maintain myself for the Lord always, but why are you saying this? There was no answer. I'm convinced the whole situation was planned and premeditated. I never felt good about him dragging his daughter or anyone into our situations. All that happened was unnecessary, maybe yes, I could've handled all this differently. I should've just been left. But the pressures of how people looked at me, the confusion in my heart and mind at the time, the pain I was enduring didn't let me think logically at the moment. This can happen to any of you! When I fought back it was in self-defense. These two people were not helpless. They were bound to corrupted mindsets and the lies they spoke, believed and received for years.

Don't feel sorry for your abuser, your abuser is not ignorant to what he or she is doing.

Some tried to accuse me of abusing him and his daughter, I just acted in self-defense and a couple of slaps were nothing compared to what I went through in their hands. Yes I should've left, but I didn't.

self-defense —Google dictionary

ˌself dəˈfens,ˌself dēˈfens/

noun

the defense of one's person or interests, especially

through the use of physical force, which is permitted in certain cases as an answer to a charge of violent crime.

Everyone has a breaking point, everyone has a limit and my breaking point and limit came at this point. Dear reader, do not let anyone abuse you, even if they claim certain disabilities that's not a justifiable excuse for abuse. You have a right to self-defense, you have a right to speak up.

Now returning to the story, I'm taken in and I was placed in a cell. I had one call and it alerted others what happened to me. While I was in there, I was treated with much compassion and protected. As the time arrived to go to central booking, the moment I stepped foot inside the computers all went down. I was taken back to the precinct where I sang worship songs in the cell as tears streamed down my cheeks. I was concerned that I had to preach that day and he knew it. As a matter of fact, he had been angry that I was asked to preach and not him.

When everything seemed up and running again they were going to take me back but now a new female cop was present with the cop that had my case. She said to me if I would've been there last night, he'd be here too. I've seen these cases. He beat you right? She turned to the cop and expressed how I was too delicate to put in that setting. She suggested they spoke to sergeant to try to keep me in cell there. It was granted to them that I wouldn't go to central booking. Hours went by and the sergeant's shift was over. He came over told me my husband was dropping the charges. He also told me his shift was over and it was a pleasure meeting me. Everything will be fine. That really touched me. Like two hours later, the cop that stood with me came in civilian clothes. I was looking at wall and singing when he opened up and said you're free.

Let's take a pause here. This all took place in July 2013, and every detail is still so vivid in my head. I cannot unscramble scrambled eggs. It be something else to be able to put scrambled eggs back in a shell, so all there is left is to add the juice, the toast and home fries and move on with life and I surely did. I have more to share in the pages to come. But I tell you putting this together hasn't been easy. I had to go back into my heart and mind and revisit the events step by step that caused me pain and that has been a great challenge. This particular one, I actually wanted to leave out of this book. The abuse had not stopped here. I could've stopped it but I caved in to his apologies and deceit. I was bound by my own deceitful heart. So, since there's so much to talk about, I wanted to leave this part out. Just so that I didn't have to remember it.

I'm not here to play a pity party and I'm not here to glorify the abuser not tear him down. But as I prayed, whether I needed to speak on this experience or not, I asked God for a sign and 4 days later in this present year 2017, after all was said and done between us he went on social media with his circle or should I say his circus and tell his suppose story. ¼ of the truth, slandering, lying and trying to intimidate me. He shared that I had been arrested and how he was so kind to drop the charges, he only shared what's convenient for his image. . It took me back to an email he once wrote me. He wrote he would put me on a platter and serve me to my enemies. I also remember him back in summer of 2013 telling me he had pastors and leaders , friends who all hated me and how they will go come together to destroy me and tarnish my image. So as I came across this video, I got the answer to my question. I included this experience here because someone needs to know they can overcome, someone needs to know they should not allow a bully and his circus to keep them from being free and I also am making a public statement that I will not allow his taunts to scare, intimidate me and stop me from putting out this book!

Being well aware that my book promo had been going out and that some people following me in my social media pages were not all for me and made him aware so he needed to come up with a defense, maybe in hopes to stop you who's reading from ever picking up this book.

As you may see and read, this relationship was very toxic and yet I stood firmly in it. I thought as a Christian I needed to endure, I thought I'd look horrible in the eyes of many with a second divorce under my belt and a broken marriage within months, I believed God could save this marriage. I prayed, I fasted, God had mercy and compassion on me, but looking back I think he would've had me walk away rather than stop trying to fix it myself. Know these kind of relationships are toxic and you should not stay in them regardless of your faith, what your uninformed pastor tells you, some pastors expect you to stay for the cause of Christ and it's caused many damages in the kingdom. You can pray from a distance, let go, let God and work on the most valuable thing right now YOU! I want some of you who like to point fingers at women who stay in these relationships to understand many women are dealing with Intimidation, guilt and are being manipulated. Some are terrified of leaving and being followed and killed. They're not stupid for staying, it's a mental cap, it's a spiritual hold, it's an emotional latch and a deceitful heart in place and by being pushy, judgmental, and angry at them, you're not going to be any sort of help. They need emotional support and to feel you're a safe place to go to and hopefully that will help them build the courage to get up and out of that situation because they feel the loving, nurturing, strong support.

I never called cops because I was afraid he'd lose his bed-bound daughter, there was guilt, I didn't leave because he threatened to hurt himself or felt the guilt again, I didn't speak up because I was afraid, manipulation and intimidation, I didn't leave because I wanted to do what was right as a wife and I loved him and love doesn't give up but that was the bondage of a deceitful heart talking to me. When I first tried to share with one female pastor about the red flags I saw while dating him, she told her husband and then they tried to throw subs at me in their church service and told him, it created a huge argument with him. I was judged so when the worst came I stood quiet for long. Should've left then but kept believing I was the change he

needed, my love was like no other. Again I never even reported him to police every time he slapped, shoved, hit, threatened... There was always an "I'm sorry, please don't call the cops," I don't want to lose my daughter and so forth.
Yet when the time came, did he have consideration? Compassion? Mercy on me? No, he set me up to have a good alibi once he abandoned me. .

I want you to realize my dear friend reading this, once a person is operating in an abusive state of mind there is no love that would keep them and change them. Unless they surrendered to God and allowed him to love them and liberate them. So are you in a toxic relationship? Does story sounds familiar to what you're facing. But you're still there. What are you waiting for? A worst experience than mine? Call the hotlines, tell your pastor, go to the hospital and find a social worker there. Pastors don't ignore the cry for help, prayerfully use wisdom, remember her emotions are sensitive, and as such give instruction without being harsh or insensitive, when someone is bound by a deceitful heart you're dealing with spiritual forces, emotional oppression. . For those who think she needs to stay because God hates divorce and he does. But he also hates abuse and abuse is a form of infidelity. The vows to each other and to God are broken when that hand that was supposed to lead and protect became the fist in her face. A woman should never be bound to a man in such circumstances of abuse. I realized over time I was married to a narcissist. I knew something was wrong, I knew everything was wrong and if I stood any further I'd probably lose myself but I remained bound, broken, confused.

My dear reader, a narcissist will not stop at anything. They will manipulate, control and deceive many with their charm. . Are you dating one? Marrying one? Married to one?

According to Lindsey Dogson in her article on businessinsider.com

7 psychological phrases to know if you're dating a narcissist

Now that you're totally depleted you are of no use to a narcissist, and so there's no reason to keep you around.

Depending on whether they're looking to get further supply from your friends and family, Anderson warns in her blog post that they may turn to them for support. You may even find none of them believe your side of the story because they're just as enchanted by the narcissist as you were. This is called a "smear campaign."

Sociopaths don't necessarily work alone either. If they're really intent on destroying you, they may rely on a gang of "flying monkeys" to make your life miserable. It's a reference to The Wizard of Oz, where the flying monkeys do all the Wicked Witch of the West's dirty work.

Some of them go along happily with the schemes because they are sociopaths themselves. Others have no idea what they're a part of because they're under the narcissistic spell.

Meet me now in chapter 11 for it didn't end here...

Notes :
_____

_____
_____
_____
_____

Chapter 11

An unending cycle I needed to end

If you ever find yourself in the wrong story leave – Unknown

Here, I am sitting on a table surrounded by ministers, colleagues, friends in Harlem. I was among those and was one of those presented with a New York State Citation award And a Borough president certificate of appreciation. I was acknowledged for the work and efforts I gave to community in our city. But I'm sitting there, wearing my friend's dress because my things were scattered. After the incident, I couldn't return home. He got exactly what he wanted, which was kicking me out the apartment. .one night I slept on beauty parlor floor, then, friend's couches and eventually all over the place. It had been just a few days and to receive such honor after being in jail was something else. I felt like Joseph. Let me not forget to mention that upon leaving the precinct, God directed me to go to the church where I was supposed to preach that Sunday and yes in flip flops, a summer dress, locked up for 14 hours prior, no makeup, here I went and the Pastor said God said I had to preach. It was glorious, the message was called " It could happen to you". God moved in such a powerful way that night and then we proceeded to a dinner party upstairs that was put together as a late wedding gift. Isn't that something? But if there's anything I learned through is

God's love, mercy, favor and power. His strength is available in your weakest moments and his hand of protection is over you when you think there is no way out. All I saw from the moment I stepped in that precinct was God's favor, at the church, God's favor, at this dinner God showed off with favor. While my name was being tarnished left to right with accusations and allegations of mental illness and abuse, God was honoring my name. It wasn't the city, it wasn't the wonderful people who nominated me? It was God! He knew what would be happening and so the devil set me up but God had set the devil up for shame.

I remember how my then husband started posting pictures of a trophy that was given to him in appreciation at an event some weeks prior. He began to put that as a default picture and was angry at the fact that people posted pics of me with my recognition from NY State Assembly. This man hated anything positive I did, he never celebrated any of my achievements and to work so hard for an alibi and now I was being acknowledged a few days later was a hit underneath his belt. I was so humbled by God's love, God's defense, and God's ways.

The days went by and I stood in different friend's homes. It was very difficult. I couldn't believe I was now homeless. I'm thankful for those who opened their hearts and their doors to me and sheltered. It was a new journey but a very difficult one as I embarked on it. Some of those who opened their doors to me couldn't understand why I still loved him, why I wanted to receive a miracle and it made some of them angry to see me go through what I was going through and still hang on. I understand it hurt them but getting angry at me, walking away because I chose to wait wasn't the right way to minister to me or anyone else. Here, I was being controlled by a man and now I felt I was being controlled by other people. I just couldn't breathe. I felt like I was losing myself and had to live to please everyone but me. Funny thing, I was also forgetting who I was. I was lost in so much pain and shame. Three months into a marriage and now homeless? Well, as the weeks went by he searched until he found me. Someone must've hinted him where I had been. When I sat in his van, very fearful, but very hopeful he got very emotional. He said to me he felt like he was losing his mind. He expressed how empty and lonely the house was without me. He said to me "Genie, I'm so bored, I go help my neighbor do things to kill time. I miss you so much, you're my best friend. "He went on to say, I want you back home, but why did you have to slap Celine? Now, she's going to make it difficult for you to come back. Talk about confusing the living day lights out of me. I replied, you know what you both did, you dragged her into this. You beat me and she touched me as well, she was in on this. How else did you want me to react? She's going to make it difficult? You're the one who wanted me out in the first place. Of course, he explained himself, said he was under pressure because of her and told me he didn't want to be without me. Silly me, thought this was God working in him, was too blind to see past what was really going on.

Look my friend, do you know how many men have said they're sorry and women believe that song and dance only to find themselves wrapped up in more pain, wasting months, years of their lives to end up losing their valuable time and some have never made it back alive. When someone is truly sorry, their apology is followed by a massive change. If change is hard for them because of habits, psychological issues, emotional issues, insecurities whatever it may be they will want to change for themselves and make a sole decision to get professional and spiritual help as well. Eventually, as time goes by and I'm not talking a few months, as time goes by you will see the fruit of their change. Yet, this is pretty rare in many cases and its best to let go, love from a distance and let God lead. But make sure it's God. God will never lead you to a place of no peace, abuse, conflict and danger. As I looked back, I see the bondage that I was in. My heart wanted what was right and what was right to me was to love him as 1 Corinthians 13 said to love:

1 Corinthians 13 (Amplified Bible)
13 If I speak with the tongues of men and of angels, but have not [a]love [for others growing out of God's love for me], then I have become only a noisy gong or a clanging cymbal [just an annoying distraction]. 2 And if I have the gift of prophecy [and speak a new message from God to the people], and understand all mysteries, and [possess] all knowledge; and if I have all [sufficient] faith so that I can remove mountains, but do not have love [reaching out to others], I am

nothing. 3 If I give all my possessions to feed the poor, and if I surrender my body [b]to be burned, but do not have love, it does me no good at all.

4 Love endures with patience and serenity, love is kind and thoughtful, and is not jealous or envious; love does not brag and is not proud or arrogant. 5 It is not rude; it is not self-seeking, it is not provoked [nor overly sensitive and easily angered]; it does not take into account a wrong endured. 6 It does not rejoice at injustice, but rejoices with the truth [when right and truth prevail]. 7 Love bears all things [regardless of what comes], believes all things [looking for the best in each one], hopes all things [remaining steadfast during difficult times], endures all things [without weakening].

8 Love never fails [it never fades nor ends]. But as for prophecies, they will pass away; as for tongues, they will cease; as for the gift of special knowledge, it will pass away. 9 For we know in part, and we prophesy in part [for our knowledge is fragmentary and incomplete]. 10 But when that which is complete and perfect comes, that which is incomplete and partial will pass away. 11 When I was a child, I talked like a child, I thought like a child, I reasoned like a child; when I became a man, I did away with childish things. 12 For now [in this time of imperfection] we see in a mirror dimly [a blurred reflection, a riddle, an enigma], but then [when the time of perfection comes we will see reality] face to face. Now I know in part [just in fragments], but then I will know fully, just as I have been fully known [by God]. 13 And now there remain:

faith [abiding trust in God and His promises], hope [confident expectation of eternal salvation], love [unselfish love for others growing out of God's love for me], these three [the choicest graces]; but the greatest of these is love.

I read this chapter everyday. I looked at it and read it verse by verse and I tell you every verse was a challenge but if I learned anything, I learned about what real love is.
No, it didn't change him. It doesn't really change the other party unless they experience this chapter for themselves in their lives and when a person is bent up on hurting another and there's no remorse, no conscious, only in them admitting they have a problem and surrendering to God completely could they understand this.
So, I waved love in his face and he didn't care. I forgave the incident and chose to love.
But I chose to love him, I chose to love his daughter but I didn't love myself enough. I didn't realize that, I didn't see I wasn't loving myself, to be quite honest I thought humbling myself and suffering the persecution was the right thing to do. He'd pick me up take me for ice cream, dinner but never bring me back home. If he did bring me home it was sneaking me in. I can't believe I let him sneak me in as if I wasn't his wife! What was I thinking? I was thinking he's sorry, I was thinking love is sacrificial and so here I was making love to him and basically being treated like a "mistress" and I thought it was right because I was married. I remember the pastor we were under counseling us and

telling me I couldn't go back there and keep doing that. He told me my marriage was broken and we went together and I shouldn't be coming to the house. But, I didn't understand. I was so fogged up with emotions and the thought somehow he was sorry that I took that to offense and was confused. One mistake I made was that my husband had other women ministers reach out to me and these ministers would tell me I couldn't deny myself. These were the same people that later spread rumors, because they believed I abused him and his daughters. That summer went by and here I was loving the person who set me up and put me in jail. I winded up in Mt. Poconos for a few weeks at some minister friend's home. The family there really loved me and offered to help me remain over there, help me get a job and help me move. I was fasting for 40 days. I had met a preacher from Texas and she had given me a powerful word and I was supposed to fast with him for 40 days. But here was my side of disobedience again. I fasted but not for him. I felt I couldn't. He'd call me, blast my cell, and accuse me of being with another man. Had ministers and friends of his reach out to me insult me threatened to end my ministry. I now know if I had fasted him God would've done something. What? Not exactly sure. But he was trying to get me to focus on me and His purpose and I was so determined to fix this man, fix this marriage I did the opposite. Eventually, he called the ministers I was with and then he spoke to me. He wanted to come out and get me with his "new" pastor, yes he even left the church we were at. I suppose he couldn't handle accountability and rather be with his popular well known friend who was a pastor.

I had just found that I was pregnant again. Life was too complicated, I was praying, I was seeking but my heart wanted what it wanted. My heart wanted a family, my heart wanted my marriage to work, my heart wanted him to love me but my heart was deceitful. My heart was so deceitful that it didn't see how illogical my thoughts were. He was demanding I returned to NY to him, but not home with him. . I left a safe place to stay at a room of a sister recommended to me. Yes, as soon as I arrived he took me to his pastor but that was the beginning of another setup. However, I didn't see that coming, I saw a husband who messed up greatly but wanted his marriage.

He made me stay at the room and he called the sister with his version of the story and made her doubt me. The stress was great and it affected me physically. Went from high risk pregnancy, ovarian cysts, anxiety you name it. But I stood in the situation. .

To make a long story short, I started going to marital counseling sessions with him and this Pastor. I was told that I needed to follow him so I left the church I was at to follow him. Submission was always thrown at me. He would always complain saying I was unsubmissive.

Eventually , this father figure pastor, who'd tell me; "Genie, look at me as a father, I'm here to help you save our marriage" one day turned to me as I showed him text of my husband calling me a prostitute and said don't come to me with gossip. He doesn't want any more counseling, speak to me about your kids or anything else but don't gossip to me about your husband. That broke me! He use to encourage me to write to him and share all that was in my heart and blindly I did. I was desperate to be heard, desperate for solutions. My husband was so close to him, he wouldn't come with me to my OB/GYN appointments, he wouldn't come to support me in anyway. Eventually, one day as I was staying in a friend's home I had to leave before management found out. I was there and her mother called him. He came in his van with a minister friend I had never met. He was rude, nasty and I felt embarrassed that we had to discuss our matters in front this man I didn't know. Next thing I knew he was parked across from a precinct. The minister and I didn't know what he was doing. Apparently, he went in said I violated an order of protection I never even knew he had. Cop came out to remove me out the van with all my belongings. That included my cat in her carrier. They took my things out the van and I had a breakdown, I ripped the order when handed to me. I was outraged that this was in place since the incident in July and here we are in beginning of September and I had no clue of it. I couldn't believe that just two days prior he took me to a hotel and spoke about fixing our marriage and here we were another set up. The minister was shocked and stopped a cab and paid for it so I could get my sons home. I was grateful for his kindness. The next day, I received a call from the Pastor and he called me to inform me that if I stepped in his church the cops would be called. This was a legal order and he couldn't violate it. I asked him "How could you side with him and allow this?" You know this is a lie Reverend. You know we've been counseling with you and this order dates back effective in July, you know I was never served. I was there in your office with him, you took us out to breakfast a couple of times, and you know this is a lie, I've never violated anything. He kept his words do not come here anymore. Read what he had in front of him and shut the door of the house of worship.

If I didn't have a relationship with God, I would've left the Lord. How much more can I resist? I forgave this man, I thought he wanted to save our marriage. He continued preaching, singing, living a double life in the pulpits meanwhile I had shut my radio station since I had gotten married, he didn't want it streaming from his home unless I transferred my program into his computer (control), he made me say no to many invitations, he abused me physically, put me in jail and now after I've forgiven him he sets me up again and this pastor is okay with that?

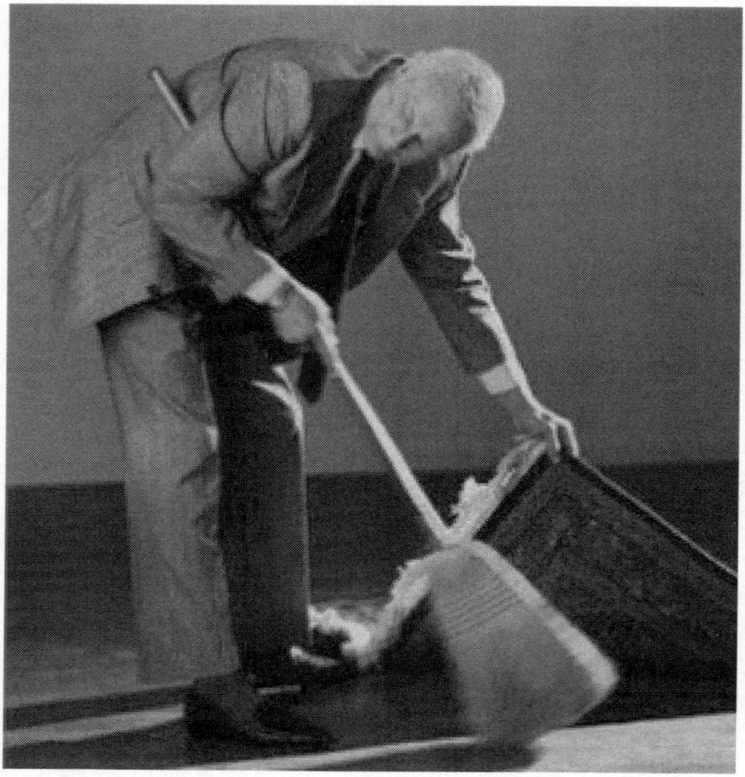

I was too ashamed to go back to the pastor where I had just been at, too ashamed to go back to my original covering from where bad been released to pastor. I felt lonely, I felt so confused. I kept getting people coming to prophesy to me who didn't even know me saying God was going to restore my marriage. The confusion was so great, the pain was so excruciating, I wanted to give up on everything.

Eventually, God took me to a little church where he placed a pastor who saw beyond all things and she took me under her wings to heal my wounded soul, pour into me and push me back out into my calling. He did come around again, he did come around my workplace, and he eventually dropped the order of protection. I wasn't eating right, I wasn't taking care of myself, I lived in distress. I had many health challenges I didn't share with anyone. I quietly hoped to die. But that little church, that Pastor, those church folks loved me and didn't leave me. I'm so thankful for them. I would've died spiritually and physically if God didn't place them in my life. I never held a baby in my arms, my dreams kept being shattered, the pain increased, I didn't care about myself, I winded up with a few health issues that had to be taken care of. Yet, in this time he continued to come back and I continued to allow him in. I kept giving him back control. So much control that managed to get me to close my social network pages. His daughter eventually called me from a private number asking me to forgive her and begged me to never tell her father about the call. Holidays came, I was there to visit them. I remember thanksgiving was a platform for him to humiliate me in front of the guest. Christmas came, I had returned to live in NJ and he came over several times. By three months he convinced me to move back to NY. He said there was no way we'd work out our marriage with me in another state. Then I came to find out that he was telling people not only that I abused him and his daughters but that I left him for a man in NJ.

Ok. That's a lot right? Rest your mind. Even I need to take a pause as I relive all these moments in my heart and mind.

Are you confused? Do you feel like you want out but your heart tells you to stay?
Are you pressured by religious beliefs? Are you feeling like there's no one to turn to and trust? Do you feel like you don't know whether you're coming or going? Are you neglecting yourself because you're obsessed with fixing the problem?

I understand. I was there. As I look back I see how my emotions were more tangled than a can of spaghetti. The feelings of abandonment and rejection were really getting the best of me. I was fighting for someone's love but he wasn't fighting for mine, he was fighting me. People on the outside looking in can see me about to hit the brick wall, but I couldn't see it. My prayer and hope is that if you're in this same situation, reading about mine back then would give you a glimpse on what's going on with you and how much you're worth. I pray this brings clarity to your thought life. Look, I meant well. I am, not ashamed of having loved someone unlovable, but if I could turn back the pages I wouldn't have stayed and allowed the abuse. I went through it, I didn't die, but could've I was visited by suicidal thoughts often, but prayed, fasted and kept myself going to church. I was a minister, a woman of authority, just had to find the courage to stand in it. Maybe you're a minister, a politician's wife, a leader of some sort and are hiding the fact that you're being abused because of what people think. Look, at the end of it all, it's your life and God didn't create you to be bound, broken and destroyed.

We have an enemy and he will scheme and use whomever it is that allows him access.

John 10:10 New International Version (NIV)

10 The thief comes only to steal and kill and destroy; I have come that they may have life, and have it to the full.

Living in an abusive relationship is not living life to the fullest. It's giving control to the enemy Himself over your life. His plans? To steal your peace, kill your dreams and destroy you!

Yes, I came out of it but before I share how, there's much more I need to say to you.
I'm putting this all out so that YOU can breathe again!

Chapter 12

The Controller

"The need for control always comes from someone that has lost it."
— Shannon L. Alder

So, here I was back living in North Newark. It was a beautiful apartment but I was very sad with everything I had already experienced. Among the things I experienced was getting robbed at gun point. Funny how they took everything I had but not my wedding rings.
Wedding rings, hhmmmm- they're round, symbolic, circles, meaning no end. While many rush to take off their rings during a separation, I didn't. I knew my vows weren't only to him, but to God. I knew separated did not mean available and I was convinced within myself at the time that this would end. That the pain would end, he'd realize how much I loved him, he would get help and we would be the biggest testimony ever.
Sadly, that eventually was not the outcome.
Separated physically, not living under same roof but still together intimately. He eventually moved me back to a basement apartment in NY, and he paid for it, he wanted me near but not in his home. He kept using his daughter as an excuse. I didn't understand, because we all made peace and put what happened behind us.

Especially me, I didn't do anything to deserve such hate. When I would ask her she'd tell me she didn't know why he was saying that. As a matter of fact Celine had traveled out of state and stood away for quite some time. So here I am moving in a basement. He had the keys, I'd often come home from work and find him working on something around the house. We were like starting over so I thought. But it was all part of him being in control for he was scheming something, you'll see, just keep reading.

At this point, not only had he forbidden me from posting anything about us in any network page, but he had also forbidden me taking pictures of him. He then went as far as saying he was closing his Facebook account and I should too. He had already blocked me from his original page and created another page where I was his only friend. He controlled all I posted, went through every one of my pictures, would tell me if he wanted a picture off and so forth. Even when he closed down that particular page, he tried to use other dummy pages to try to provoke me to flirt. I always caught on to him and he would get angry. He knew every move I made, using other people to watch my every post and every move. A time came when he told me that it was either Facebook or him and forced me to close my Facebook account.

If I did anything opposite to what he was asking me to, he'd threaten to disappear.

He'd get crazy and begin yelling and I was so afraid of him hitting me again, and I did my best to avoid it at all cost. So it was like a yes sir, OK sir, kind of life. He argued over things such as the last name Caraballo being on my mailbox. That was my last name since 1993 and after the first divorce, I never planned to remarry and then when I did want to change my last name back to my real maiden name, all kind of situations aroused because of typos not corrected when I was a child, anyway, he hated that name. I still received mail with that name and he wanted me to just be Santos. Which, BY the way this issue of control carried out to our divorce. I wanted the right to use Santos at the moment because of all my school financial papers but he purposely had Caraballo written in my decree as the surname to return to. Because of some typos on birth certificate that clashes with decree I can't return to my maiden name" Rivera" just yet. He knew this but for some reason he wanted to see me return to my first ex-husbands name "Caraballo." . As time went by I realized the apt was rat infested, not one rat but a few rats. I had water ceiling leaks, sewer backups, you name it and it was ok with him that I go through this. He would tell me it wasn't time yet to live together again. Meanwhile, I'd cook, he'd come over and he would post on his Facebook and tell others he was single, even worst that he was getting a divorce. The physical abuse stopped, but now I began to deal with a controlling husband, very intimidating and I sought refuge in God but couldn't seem to be able to let go. Often times, he'd say things like if I wanted to, I could put you in a body bag and make you disappear or he'd say he felt like dying, no one cares, everyone was a hypocrite. He really played on my emotions and manipulated them to the core.

There's some of you who may not be in a physically abusive situation, but being controlled and manipulated is also an abuse. Some people would tell me, consider his past, he was wounded and he's insecure. However, considering him almost destroyed me. I was so unhappy. As time has gone by and I look back, I see many things I couldn't see then. I also have educated myself more on the topic of abuse. Understanding what I survived has been helpful in the healing process. Here is some valuable information about abuse I came across on Cedar Network. The writer defines this kind of abuse as "Coercive Control."

According to this article, "Coercive control is a term developed by Evan Stark to help us understand domestic abuse as more than a "fight." It is a pattern of behavior which seeks to take away the victim's liberty or freedom, to strip away their sense of self. It is not just women's bodily integrity which is violated but also their human rights."

It goes further on to say; in this model, violence is used (or not) alongside a range of other tactics – isolation, degradation, mind-games, and the micro-regulation of everyday life (monitoring phone calls, dress, food consumption, social activity, etc.). The perpetrator creates a world in which the victim is constantly monitored and criticized; every move is checked against an unpredictable, ever-changing, unknowable 'rule-book.'

The rules are based on the perpetrator's stereotyped

view of how his partner should behave toward him, rules about how she cooks, house-keeps, mother's, performs sexually and socializes.

For more information go to
https://www.cedarnetwork.org.uk/about/supporting-recovery/what-is-domestic-abuse/what-is-coercive-control/

Because No one needs to live like this!
I did anyway! The control went crazy ! He did what he had to do to cover his tracks. Infidelity was the new spewing thing. He'd be intimate with me one night and the next with another. I must tell you that my prayer life kept me. I prayed and sometimes fasted for days. Through every fast, God will expose something else. Now, I know the Lord was revealing to me what was in the dark so that I wouldn't stay in it. But I chose to stay and fight for the marriage. In my heart, it was a marriage, in his and with his actions, it was a broken covenant. I don't even think it ever meant anything to him. Starting a relationship with me and marrying me was just a way of him cleaning his last reputation. Last marriage exposed who he was to many , but this time he wanted to build up a new case against a new woman so that he can appear clean before the people's eyes. He was concerned about the rumors throughout the years of him being abusive . There's just one thing he forgot, that only works with those that carry the same darkness as he did and lacked discernment. Those who were under the narcissistic spell.
Many female pastors fell in his web of deceit and

control. I remember one particular pastor that I approached respectfully, but truthfully. I had been fasting, and I found a woman's picture wearing a baby doll in his computer files. A week later as I ended a fast, without even looking, the information came to me. He had been lying about helping an old pastor. Every time I offered to give a hand, he said no this is among men. When it all came to light, I found out that he was helping a female pastor who looked just like the woman in the pic. Yes, I know this is hard for some of you to read. They are some of you that are so religious, saving image and you want to keep sweeping the dirt in the churches underneath the carpet. But God has instructed me to pull your carpets up and show the dirt. Yes, some of you are thinking how many who hate church will read this and be discouraged. But how about being truthful and not letting your altars remain polluted? Look, no one is perfect. We all fall short, but to know something is a sin and allow it to keep going on is horrible. I could write a book alone on the dirt underneath the carpets. God calls us to repentance.

Now, if I approached her respectfully, why did she blocked me? It went as far as that when she finally returned the call, she didn't have a civil talk with me. She told me off. Wait, I was the wife, and she was telling me off. She had no idea that she was on speakerphone and I had a witness. As time went on, I continued to fast. I wanted to know more even if it hurt. Now mind you, if I could turn back the hands on the clock, I'd revisit and tell me – Hey Genie, isn't enough, enough? He's not changing. Walk away, girl run! But I didn't. One day I was on the train on my way to a meeting when I felt this ball of fire in my stomach, and I heard in my spirit get off, walk and pray in the spirit, I'm going to show you something. I was shaking, it became intense such that I had to call the evangelist that was waiting for me, and she started praying. I ran into his van and long story short, he was in that pastor's house. Was it innocent? Well, if it was, she didn't have to threaten me, and he didn't have to go lie and get an order of protection so that I wouldn't track him down. God even placed a policeman to speak with me in the spot and he gave me great advice. So, I also got an order against him. I showed all the emails with threats at the precinct, and when the day finally came; June 24th, 2014, we both dropped the charges. I walked away and he ran after me. I just wanted to be left alone but he grabbed my arm and said, "Genie, I do love you. Give me time. All in time." What was that about? Well, back then I thought maybe answered prayer, now I know it was control!

So, let's talk. How are you being controlled? Do you think this is anyway to live? What's keeping you there?

I want you to think about these questions and write them down right below.

_____
_____
_____
_____

———————

OK now. I want you to think about what you just wrote. Reflect on it and look in the mirror.

Mirror, Mirror on the wall. Who deserves to be happy

above all?

You dear reader. You deserve to be happy, and it's time to come up with a plan, build up the courage you need, trust in God and be the happiest of all!

Notes :

_____

_____

_____

_____

Chapter 13

Journey through the truth

As I begun this book, much information and heartfelt truths about my experience have been shared, most not in chronological order so that we can focus on certain elements of abusive situations. Nevertheless, the last few chapters are in chronological order, and its content has been relived by me and reliving it in my mind and heart has been a whole new process of healing, revelation, and insight. In the last chapter, I spoke about Coercive control and how I was living under it. You may be asking, so after the physical abuse, the set ups, the control, there's more? Yes, it didn't end in the previous chapter. Even though my decision to stay wasn't anything I would advise myself if I could go back in a time machine now, I must say it took lots of courage, and the pain led me to seek God out more. Many may not understand also that there was a purpose with me in all this. When I dropped those charges (which is not my advice to anyone unless a specific thing happens like what happened to me) I dropped them because I felt it in my spirit, a pastor told me she felt I should, and a neighbor called me crying in middle of doing dishes and said the Lord made her feel I need to drop them. This may not make sense, but this was part of God's plan at this point to reveal and expose more. When I dropped the charges, to keep the peace, I was ready to walk away. He, as I mentioned in the previous chapter, ran after me to tell me he loved me and so forth. That same night, he showed up banging on my door. I thought for a moment that it meant God was going to work it out. He started coming every day that week except for Friday and he came by Saturday and Sunday as well. Yes, we made up, I decided to forgive him again, and that Sunday, he asked me to meet him outside by the avenue. When I got in the van, I remember he had his blue suit and white shirt, very dapper and very drunk! He grabbed me like an animal to kiss me and wanted a liquor store. He took off before I could say anything and I saw my life flash before my eyes because of how he was driving intoxicated. He kept saying he was a bad boy among other things as he ran into a liquor store to get a bottle of cognac. I was so terrified such that I was frozen in the passenger seat. He parked by the Happyland memorial monument in Southern Blvd and began to say he wanted to end his life. I wanted to catch a cab home, but here was guilt again.

What if I left and he killed himself? He got out of the van, came back in and wanted to force me to drink with him. I tasted it so he'd leave me alone, I was scared, but I refused to drink. He pulled me by my hair and kept saying, "I married you, I gave you my last name, I married you. I loved you Genie, I loved you." I didn't understand why he was doing that but if he loved me, why the lies, the abuse, the set ups? Why all this? I begged him to let go of my hair. He let go and I

was shaking. He drove me back home. I suggested that he come in and drink coffee, have his rest and sober up. Instead, he had me go to the bakery and get him coffee and then he left. He called me around 20 minutes later and said, baby I'm home. Going to bed. Like 15 minutes after that call, the ministry phone rang. A female voice abruptly asks "are you Genie? Pastor Genie?" And I said "yes." She went on to say, tell your ex-husband to stop calling me and my pastor with restricted number.. I broke up with him. At that moment I said first of calm your voice down, we're still married, who are you?
She went on to explain he showed her some divorce papers,.I said divorce papers? We're not in a divorce process? She explained every detail how they met in this particular church in the South Bronx. They met in the church of the Pastor I previously mentioned. He would go see the pastor, try to lure her and step out to supposedly check on his daughters but would go to see her church member to have sex with her. When I say prayer works, it works. When I say fasting is powerful, it is. Not only was all this being revealed, but I didn't Spazz out! Just imagine you get a call from a 29-year-old young woman who's confessing to you everything about her sexual open relationship with your husband. To prove to you that she's not lying she tells you what he was wearing earlier in the day and you saw him in that same outfit. To make it worst, she describes his body, birthmarks, tattoos, how he took her into intimacy and you just have to pause her there. Like hey wait that's enough! Here I was listening to this. My 50-year-old husband had an affair with a 29-year-old and

was wooing her pastor, whom happened to be the one to tell me off and call me crazy on the phone. To top it off, she was in recovery and with a baby daddy in jail. I listened, I shared the truth of the matter and when asked if I loved him and why , I took her to the book of Hosea. I ministered to her and she wanted to see what I looked like. She had only seen a picture of my state ID which he had copies off. Yes he made copies, opened mail, did many things. She even told me about how he opened every piece of mail I still received in the home. I sent her one of my videos and she was touched and said to me; "You're so beautiful, what's wrong with this man?" She apologized for everything. By the next day, Monday morning, she mustered up the courage to not only tell her pastor the truth but to go with her and sit with his pastor and confess all that had been happening. Did it change anything? No. But I did respect that she did that. She owned up to her mistakes and had a greater conviction than any of the other women. Yes, there were many. Including several exes that I didn't understand, if he abused them why did they want him back? I remember him coming home to me after the whole truth unveiled. I didn't know how to respond. I had so much Jesus in me that I just listened to that still small voice. Stay calm, make coffee as usual, give him his favorite crackers and butter and take off his shoes. Take off his what? Serious? But at this point it was it a deceitful heart or was it a victory march? I had made many wrong turns but at this point, I was sure this was God, and I had to obey. That crazy action led me to my freedom. Humility led me to my peace. God knew I wasn't going to have the guts to walk out yet, so he worked with my sensitivity and heart. This made him begin to open up and say things that were incredibly unbelievable.

I remember him taking me to his home, what at one time was my home. We watched movies, I didn't bring anything up. But he kept talking, he said in his chair and expressed how he was helping her and she was ungrateful. I couldn't believe he had the nerve to sit there and justify his affair and call her ungrateful for speaking out. He said her tongue deserved to be cut off. He went on and on expressing his anger, not only toward her, but toward his last ex-wife as well, toward church friends and on and on. He then said if I kill one, I might as well finish all that hurt me off. But I'm too old to do that. At that point, I played a worship song and asked him to listen. I was afraid of saying anything else that would make him take all of that anger on me. I remember going into the bathroom just to speak to the Lord. He wanted intimacy and rejection wasn't what he expected. I didn't want to be touched. How many betrayals could I take? How could it be true that God could restore us? This man didn't want God? As I looked around the apartment, I saw everything she described including her gifts to him.

Time went by and he was extra nice and visiting me, being with me, sharing and for a moment I thought ok this is it. I mean, there are marriages I've seen bounce back and that are really healed by God why couldn't mine be healed? I was bound by a false sense of hope. God was showing me all the reasons why it was OK to let this man go peacefully. Wasn't I more valuable than what he made me to be? That Wonder Woman

syndrome had me blind. I kept thinking this unconditional love as of the one from Hosea to Gomer will bring him back to his senses. Not!
If there is anything though I must say I learned through this time was God's unconditional love for me and how His love was relentless. I learned to love deeply and passionately but as time has gone by I've learned that my wine was a big spill in this man's case for he wasn't receiving it. There's a time, a place for that kind of love and it wasn't with him. Don't get me wrong, I don't regret loving him in this time. I learned a lot about loving your enemies. There's so much strength found in loving he who doesn't love you back and praying for them but please do that from a distant. It is not healthy to stay in situations that mess with your thinking and expose you to the manipulation of someone who's trying to rub the feces they've stepped on you.

I still believe that my case was really unique and God dealt with me with such love and grace and taught me as I went along many lessons, even when I wasn't picking up and leaving as I had every right to do. Throughout those years there was so much more I haven't mentioned, degrading emails , the times he asked me for sensual pics to think of me when I wasn't around and because I was his wife and I was bent up on doing what I had to do I sent him whatever he wanted. He changed his number and my only way to contact was email every day and instill stood. When your heart is deceived by fear, insecurity, confusion it paralyses your right thinking. I didn't think he'd later insult me right after asking for the pics, he even went around telling people I was harassing him with perversion. Every time, something he said got to my ears I would hurt deeply, and would lose focus.

But here we were, I had put up with 2 ½ years of craziness. I was losing myself. I had no joy. People who knew me well would reach me and say Genie I see it all over your face in your videos, in your pictures, what's going on? I walked on eggshells. Didn't know if today was a good day but tomorrow a bad one. I was surrounded by others who believed God could save my marriage. Honestly, that's all I wanted to hear. But I was slowly missing what God was trying to do. Then the day came. The day it was over.

We're almost winding down and out this book. As you may see, I had a huge battlefield in the mind. Confusion was ruling my heart. I just hung on to God hates divorce and He does. There's no perfect couple and differences can be worked out. The Holy Spirit can transform anything and anyone. But I see this was deeper than just a troubled man, this was a narcissist situation.

This man had visible psychological problems and knew how to camouflage them with his charm and make it seem like I was the crazy one. For the record, I've never had a mental condition. That alone is a miracle after all I've been through. I was brave enough to see professionals for evaluations whenever something traumatic happened in my life, and God has blessed this mind of mine with sanity and stability. After this relationship, I should've been nuts! Again, one thing I did right through it all was live a life of prayer. Live a full relationship with my Heavenly Father who wasn't shocked at my sometimes stubborn, sometimes too sensitive, too scared, too giving self. He knew, I really cared and He worked patiently with me to put all things into the right perspective.

Exodus 34:6
Then the LORD passed by in front of him and proclaimed, "The LORD, the LORD God, compassionate and gracious, slow to anger, and abounding in loving-kindness and truth;

Isaiah 30:18
Therefore the LORD longs to be gracious to you, And therefore He waits on high to have compassion on you For the LORD is a God of justice; How blessed are all those who long for Him.

When the Narcissists family seeks to attack your credibility to protect the Narcissist, know that they are enablers. They have been repeatedly manipulated and used by the Narcissist. Enablers protect the bad things that the Narcissist has done and have the potential to blame or accuse you if the Narcissist begins to act out. He could be the most abusive person in the world but if he has enablers, it makes him feel more powerful because no one is telling him to stop.

Notes to self :

_____

_____

_____

_____

Chapter 14

Abandoned or Released?

On November 18, 2014, I had a terrible cough and had evening classes at my college and was getting ready when he called. Three weeks had gone by and I had not heard from him. I had gotten used to his disappearing acts and his infidelity that I didn't stress it, just kept doing what I had to do and praying. He calls me as if nothing happened, I didn't start questioning, I didn't care to ask where he had been, instead I just said, "Hey babe, I missed you, how are you?" We got into a conversation and he kept hearing me cough and suggested I didn't go to school feeling under the weather. I mentioned I had to go outside regardless to get some things I needed. He insisted I should stay, asked me if I had cough medicine, tea and honey, proceeded in asking what was it I needed from the store and said I'll see you in a little bit, stay home, I remember that day as if it was yesterday. He came over with all the things I needed, including medicine, honey, and tea. He had movies with him. I'm not a TV person or movie buff, but I always watched movies with him. Whenever he came over, we watched movies, ate and spent special moments. In spite of all that had been going on, this is what we always do repeatedly. This was one of the reasons why it was hard at times to detach as well. Sometimes we stay because we get so used to that person's company and

our routine with them. Life adjusts around that one good moment a week and ignore all the bad moments the rest of the week.
We spent that whole afternoon and evening together. He was so attentive and kind. Sort of like when we first started our relationship where he flooded me with attention and did random acts of kindness. I remember as he sat by the table, he kept his head down as he spoke to me and I touched his face and said, "Nothing you could ever do will make me love you less." He shook his head and in a low voice said, "Crazy." Everything ended so nice, there was friendship, there was romance, and there was who I had fallen in love with. I was so overtaken by recognizing him at this time that I surely thought I have arrived. This is it. He won't abuse me anymore. It paid off going through all I have gone through and enduring. As he left, he gave me the biggest hug and said, "I love you baby." The next day he called me in the am to ask me a question about some medical appointment. I was like his personal secretary at times. So, I took the opportunity to ask, babe what are our plans for thanksgiving? He said I don't know Genie, I don't know. He had to go and hung up. I never saw him again, never heard from him again.
 It was at this time where the biggest challenge came to me. For months I had been having visions of me pastoring and God spoke twice between the months of October and November through His vessels about my pastoring. I had been in ministry for 17 years and in that time had experienced being an interim pastor but to be the Senior Pastor of a work at this time without

my marriage being restored, I didn't see that happening. However, a lot led to it and on December 5th, 2014, I opened the doors to "The Well Christian Center Inc" in the County of the Bronx, NY. That's a whole other story for another book.

However, in this time I had to deal with unanswered emails, blocked number and no idea why he wasn't responding. January came, and he finally replied with an email. Attached to the email was a Divorce decree. I couldn't believe it, how much more harm was he going to do? Though being broken away from him was probably the best thing for me, this man who claimed to be a minister abused me physically, emotionally, mentally and knew he had a stronghold on me now appeared to have had filed for a divorce. Now, as many couples who argue and in anger say I'm divorcing you, he had said that in the midst of his control and intimidation whenever he didn't get his way about something. But here I was going to court and finding out that this divorce had been filed a year earlier and his friend's daughter had signed the affidavit as if she delivered it to me in my workplace. Now how many of you know that God don't side with lies. God made a way for me to bring this back to the courts. First off, I never abandoned him, I didn't want that to be on a divorce record, and I deserved a fair chance to be heard. After all, I put up with all the junk given to me, and I deserved to fight for my rights. God's favor was over me. I had a letter from my former boss stating the truth. My former boss was a man of God and wasn't standing for such lie that I was served such notice at my workplace and didn't comply with the court orders.

The divorce was annulled. I had mercy on the lady who signed the affidavit lying only because of her mother and because he wasn't going to pay the consequences, she was and she had enough trouble with the law. So, we were still married. However, he showed that annulled decree to women and wooed them into his net. If he wanted a divorce, so be it. But do things right. Even in that process, he reached out and I still tried to fix it. My mind and heart was so bound by the lie that he will change and he will return a different man and I didn't see past that.

He had me install Skype so he can video chat, we did that a few times. He'd email me insults. Terrible ones, very abusive, Putting me down in a very vulgar language and then he'd send me emails with videos of love songs. One email right before the court date said, "There's no love like yours." I'd sent emails back, pleading with him, trying to minister to his heart, trying to have peace but it backfired. Our divorce was finally sealed by July 2016.

Was all this ending process painful? Yes, indeed. Did I get anything awarded from the divorce? No, I didn't fight for it. David didn't kill Saul when he had the chance to. I had enough evidence sent to me from sources about him and how he sleeps around and I didn't care anymore. Alimony? He lived off his two daughters benefit checks, anything he did get on the side was maybe from selling something. But he didn't work . I lost all the storage he promised to pay and had to start from scratch but know what? I gained back my sense of self. It is now that I understand God had to allow things to wind down and wind me out that way

or I would've died trying to fix things.
It is now that I understand that if I had remained in his home, he would've probably killed me. It is now that I appreciate that God had him just walk away.
He didn't even serve me the divorce decree. God moved a servant of His who worked in the court to call me and tell me she saw the paperwork done. I was privileged to go into that court building and have the woman of God embraced me and prayed for me in her office as I obtained those papers. The first day I cried a little. But my tears seemed to be of relief. The second day, I looked at my rings for the last time on my finger and said Lord I've completed my part of the vow with you. I took them off, and I felt a relief. I was able to breathe again.
I learned many valuable lessons from this whole ordeal and made mistakes along the way in order to learn them. Ever since I was released I have begun to accomplish things I never thought I would and catch up with projects that were on hold while married to a man who controlled my every move. I wish at times I didn't live that, but I'm grateful that I can share this with you who feel trapped in that toxic relationship. I want you to learn from my mistakes, be courageous and fight for what's valuable to YOU!
Now, let me make this clear, I'm not saying you shouldn't believe that your marriage could be restored. Marriages have ups and downs and the only perfection in a marriage is Christ in the center.
But again, if it's an abusive, dangerous situation come out of it. That thought of for the sake of the kids doesn't work. My kids remember things I tried to hide

when I was in my first marriage and I can't even imagine how much hurt their little hearts carried while I thought I was hiding the negativity in that marriage away. Kids do know, do notice and do feel. So, for the sake of the kids get a plan going. They shouldn't have to live through the mayhem.

God set me free by ripping him off as you rip off a bandage that's gonna hurt when stuck to skin and hair. That's how he dealt with me but everyone is different. You may be in a worst scenario and reading this book is Gods message to you.

You may say but how do I start?

Let's put a plan in action. Today is the start of you Breathing again.

Chapter 15

Plan to Breathe Again

No one deserves to live life in oppression. God has called us to peace. God's desire is that we live at peace with everyone. It is time you take a good look at yourself in the mirror and say I deserve to live in peace. This person doesn't produce peace for me and so I must take the scissors and cut the strings.

Hebrews 12:14 (NLT) - Work at living in peace with everyone...
Romans 12:18 (NLT) - Do all that you can to live in peace with everyone.

Okay, now how would you plan your exit?

Make sure you have a safe place to go. I suggest you're careful with trusting anyone in his circle.
Have a list of people that you consider to be "safe" contacts so you will have someone you can call or go to for help. Again, be selective. Use discernment.
Avoid people close to the abuser. In my experience they turned on me and were part of the set ups.
Make a list of important phone numbers and memorize them. We have gotten to use to saving numbers in our devices and if they're batteries are

dead, there's trouble.

Make sure you always have a battery power pack, your chargers to your phone and even purchase phone cards in case you have to use a public phone and have no change.

Create a secret word or sign that you can use so that your family, friends or co-workers will know you need them to call for help. Something you can text or say to them over the phone.

What if he catches you? Plan out what you will say to him if he become abusive or violent. Remember you don't have to live in fear. Take control of your life.

You need to find somewhere to go. If you can't afford a place find a friend or family member who will allow you to stay with them until you are able to get a place of your own. Or go to court, dial 911 and have them to remove him from the home. You are able to do this by filing for divorce and petitioning the court for exclusive rights to the marital home. The down side with this strategy is that he will know where you are. You are safer leaving and finding safety elsewhere.

If you had joint bank accounts, don't manage money from there. Get your own account and set it up with a bit of money before you leave. DO NOT set up a new account in the same bank you have a joint account with him. Find a new bank, close to the location you will be living.

Where you're getting money from. If he's a control freak and doesn't let you have money. If you work, deposit some of your salary in your new bank account. When you are ready to go, take your rings and pawn it! Sell your Wedding Dress! Sell/pawn anything you can

get your hands on before you go.
Contact your local women's crisis center and find out how to obtain an attorney or Legal aid services, counseling etc. Every state is different but the help is available to you.

Most of all, make sure you are in tune with the Lord. If your abusive husband attends the same church with you and they're overlooking the abuse, siding with him or pressuring you to stay in danger by manipulating the scriptures then I suggest you find a church elsewhere where you can have peace at a brand new start. If he's well known as what happened to me stay away from that circle, chances are he will still try to control you and find you through their eyes.

Whatever you do just don't stop worshipping and seeking the Lord. Because it is only Him who can get you through this time, and it is Him who has the final outcome lined up in his plan.

"Fear is the glue that keeps you stuck. Faith is the solvent that sets you free."
— Shannon L. Alder

Maybe you're saying I want to leave, but I got a prophetic word. Look, I believe in the gifts of the spirit and operate in the prophetic and word of knowledge by God's grace myself. But let me make this clear. So, I was unhappy in my marriage, abused and part of me holding on was because I was believing in prophetic word! Remember that God still speaks today, but we must be careful with what we're listening to, what is coming out of the mouth of the prophet. We must be careful that every prophetic word aligns with the word of God!!

God can do anything, nothing is impossible for Him. Thus, His will is perfect and I refuse to believe He will have you stay in a situation where you could lose your sanity, your life. I see this now. If God really spoke, He's gonna do it in His time. He does not need your help. I've seen marriages get back together after 10 years of separation or divorce and I'm astonished by the transformation. Nevertheless, that is not everyone's happy ending.
Your happy ending may be starting a new beginning away from the turbulent life you have been living.

Jeremiah 29:11 (AMP).

11For I know the plans and thoughts that I have for you,' says the Lord, 'plans for peace and well-being and not for disaster, to give you a future and a hope.

Do you have peace? Isn't God interested in your well-being? Doesn't God have a plan for your future? Would He put you in a place of hopelessness?

Note to self:
_____
_____

_____
_____

_____
_____

_____
_____

_____
_____

_____
_____

"Never worry what others say when you walk away from all the drama. Be grateful you had the strength and courage to stay out of the conflict and be at peace with your choices."
— Elle Sommer

Write your own prayer to God he's ready to answer and deliver you.

_____

Chapter 16

He thought he'd keep me bound, broken, and destroyed

It was the summer of 2017 and I was on a call speaking to a minister, when she switches the subject to tell me she had heard that my ex-husbands liver issue has no remedy. According to what she had heard, he had been admitted to a hospital. Someone else told me as well and I came across a picture of him laid up in the hospital bed. My heart felt saddened for this man who had abused me, abandoned me and had no compassion for me. A man who after leaving me, contacted several ministers and their churches to defame my name. Yet, in this time that I have been alone, I had accomplished many things- school, church, written books and the greatest of all is that I had a peace of mind.
However, I'll end this book with the importance of guarding your heart. I'm not the type of person to hold a grudge, nor am I the type of person to wish bad on anybody. But I've become the type of person that don't tolerate nonsense.

I however, felt so bad about his condition. I happened to have his new number and I thought well, it's been over, he's sick , let me wish him well and remind him of God's love. Long story short that wasn't a good idea. Making peace with an abuser, wishing him well is a no, no.

The moment he knew it was me texting him, he got very hostile. It was already September 2017, and was in the middle of writing this book and it was 11:30pm when my phone is going off. I saw it was him. Again, my intentions were to wish him well, I was pretty sad because of the picture I saw of him. I only pray he gets his heart right with the Lord. But this man I once loved and wouldn't give up on doesn't have a place in my heart anymore. As a Christian, I care for people and there's strength in praying for those that persecute and hate you. Some people are humbled by circumstances and others are like pharaoh and he is definitely a pharaoh.

When I saw my phone ringing, I didn't pick up the call. He continued blasting it and so I texted him asking him to not call. Explained I was concerned about his health back then but I don't desire to speak with him, please don't call I told him. I wished him God's best and he said good night and that was it. A little while later, his daughter Celine calls, I didn't recognize the number, I answered, and she blankly accused me of calling her father and threatened me then hung up. I immediately texted her that this should be the last time she reached me, etc. I thought of filing a police report but said to myself I have nothing to do with them, let God handle them.

I learned that the past is left in the past. I also learned that when you trust God, He will defend you and He will remove the affections in your heart that don't belong to that certain individual. I'm over him, over his family over his flying monkeys. As I said earlier, he even went on a live video to degrade me and share his redemption story before this book came out. The same minister that shared his condition with me as I mentioned earlier was the same woman who interviewed him, what a shame . I don't know what her agenda was , but Oprah Winfrey sure didn't hurt others to get to where she is at the moment. I've been divorced for over a year now and this man is still relentlessly trying to stop me from living the life God has granted me. The problem here is this. I might still care for others because I'm not a cold-hearted fish, but I'm not that same fearful, intimidated, confused, broken, and bound Genie anymore. I've accomplished so much, I'm surrounded by so many wonderful people. My mindset is different and this book wasn't a tell all, tear up book. But when someone is trying to cover their image, a book like this would make them wanna do all sorts of things to stop you.

I twice told him, this will be a testimony and I will write a book about it. I won't get a dummy page like your exes did, or call the Assemblies of God, knock on every church door. I have the power of a microphone behind a radio, I have the power of writing and the power of sharing with others that they may not be deceived. He threatened he will eliminate me and therefore I'm putting it in writing. That any attempts against my life he'd be the first suspect. He also threatened to take every special personal photo he had of me while I was his wife and publish it, even sell my pictures to some Russian market. This book shouldn't be a surprise to my former abuser but I pray that if he reads it that the conviction of the Holy Spirit will take place in his heart. I pray he will allow God to heal him and deliver him for his sake. His idea of lying to his daughter back in September and having her insult me was to paralyze me again. His idea of the video and speaking of me without mentioning my name but everyone in his network knows who he was married to was an idea to make me back out of this book. He was sending a message to me, but I'm not bound, broken, and destroyed.

I'm not that Genie that stood quiet. The thoughts came, fear for my life. This man is not in his right mind but then I know that if God led me to this, He will surely get me through it. This book is a tool of encouragement and a voice to say to many women, especially women leaders, different ranks, you're not alone and you too can stand and speak up. He can't hurt you anymore than what you let him.
I'm done with a life of abuse, I stalled at chapter 8 for weeks, thinking, "Lord he's gonna hurt me" but I shook it off. No, he has no more control of me! There is so much more I could share but maybe in a sequel as the Lord leads. I just pray my transparency will reach you who is or has been on this same journey. Today I can breathe again, today I am me , myself and I and I am accomplishing many of God's purposes. The greatest of them at this moment, freeing many hearts from lies, abuse and destruction through the pages of this book. I'm free to be me, free to wear that red lipstick he complained about, free to have apple juice

after 11pm without him forbidding me, free to accept a speaking invitation without him accusing me of an affair with the pastors, free to love people!

John 10:10 - The thief comes only to steal and kill and destroy; I have come that they may have life, and have it to the full.

He thought he'd keep me bound, broken, and destroyed
but I'm breathing again & so can you!

So here's to new paths, new journeys, new things!

You too can breathe again!

Forget the former things; do not dwell on the past. See, I am doing a new thing!
Isaiah 43:18,19

List of Resources

By: M.Arslan | 05 , Mar 2013 | Elephant
http://www.liveanimalslist.com/mammals/average-size-of-an-elephant.php
Cambridge dictionary

Compassionpower.com

https://www.cedarnetwork.org.uk
Article written by : https:www.huffingtonpost.com/

Cambridge dictionary "Walking on egg shells"
Compassionpower.com

Female Suicide and Domestic Violence - Criminaljustice.iresearchnet.com
"He's a great guy; 7 Excuses Women Consistently Make for Their Horrible Boyfriends by Jenn Chan for "Elite Daily" 2014/22/8
Elitedaily.com

Gary Thomas "Enough is Enough" Garythomas.com 2016/29/11

Mack Lamouse "When Enough is Enough"-How to End an Abusive Relationship

Spotcleaning- Cudneys.com
Darlene Lancers blog www.psychologytoday
Lindsey Dogson -7 psychological phrases to know if you're dating a narcissist
Businessinsider.com

Coercive Control by Evan Stark

To you who have abused a woman, I want to remind you that you were knitted in your mother's womb.
You probably have sisters, daughters and the obvious there was a grandmother and great granny and aunts.
Maybe you never knew your mother, maybe life has been tough with you, but I want to tell you that you must
get past that hurt and not pour out your hurts, mistakes, failures on another human being. Same thing for a woman, without a dad's seed, you wouldn't have being in existence. Maybe it was your dad who hurt you, but you might have sons, uncles, cousins, etc. there's a saying hurt people hurt people but that doesn't have to be you. Look at your hands, men how wonderfully made you were in Gods image. Next time you lift up that hand, that fist, please think what if God lifted HIS against you. But instead He sent His son to die and make a way. Now don't make any mistakes, God sees it all and there's consequences for your actions. However, I want to encourage you to put that down, take your pain to the cross. Get professional and spiritual help and know that yes your life can be transformed if YOU choose to allow him to transform you.

No one owes you anything. You owe it to yourself to set yourself free from the bondage that has created a living hell inside your heart and mind and a living hell to those you have victimized.

If you're tired of abusing women, just cry out right now and say Lord I've hurt, I've destroyed, I've sabotaged the good people you placed in my life. I've sabotaged my own life and I want to put an end to it. I invite you into my life, invade my space. Holy Spirit, transform me and lead me to the right direction. Rescue me and forgive me for all I've done. I choose to let go of my hurts, my mind, and my heart is yours. Lord Jesus reign in me. Amen.

Now, don't be embarrassed, seek out pastoral help and see out wellness. Seek out therapy, support groups and if you're running from the law, turn yourself in and let God be the judge. Start afresh, God can turn any Saul into a Paul.
God bless.

For resources near you. Email us at: thewellelpozo@gmail.

About the Author

Pastor Genie Santos (Rivera) Is the Founder and Senior Pastor of The Well Christian Center inc, founded and started in the Bronx, NY and currently in The East Village NYC . Pastor Genie gave her heart to Jesus on Nov 11, 1985. She has been serving in evangelistic ministry for the past 20 years, as her passion becomes greater and greater she shares many of her experiences with different audiences with the goal of getting them to understand Salvation, receive healing and deliverance and enjoy life on Earth in His presence by fulfilling His purposes. Pastor Genie is also the founder of online Christian radio station; www.Goodradiostation.com, author of three other books; conference speaker, chaplain, and wears many hats. Her most priced and cherished call is the one of motherhood and grandma hood. She's a mother of 4 young adults and grandmother to two precious children. If you'd like to contact Pastor Genie you may email her at Thewellelpozo@gmail.com. You may also follow her on:

Follow Pastor Genie Santos on:

Facebook YouTube Instagram

Collect them all!
Makes a great witnessing tool!
Available on Amazon.com

Besos y Hugs
Love Notes from God
GENIE SANTOS

"Pearl Drops"
GENIE SANTOS

My Psalms
Genie Santos

Made in the USA
Columbia, SC
15 October 2021